THE WAY OF THE CHAMPION

Lessons from Sun Tzu's *The Art of War* and other Tao Wisdom *for Sports & Life*

JERRY LYNCH, Ph.D.
With the Collaboration of
CHUNGLIANG AL HUANG

TUTTLE Publishing

Tokyo | Rutland, Vermont | Singapore

The Tuttle Story: "Books to Span the East and West"

Most people are surprised to learn that the world's largest publisher of books on Asia had its humble beginnings in the tiny American state of Vermont. The company's founder, Charles E. Tuttle, belonged to a New England family steeped in publishing. And his first love was naturally books—especially old and rare editions.

Immediately after WW II, serving in Tokyo under General Douglas MacArthur, Tuttle was tasked with reviving the Japanese publishing industry. He later founded the Charles E. Tuttle Publishing Company, which thrives today as one of the world's leading independent publishers.

Though a westerner, Tuttle was hugely instrumental in bringing a knowledge of Japan and Asia to a world hungry for information about the East. By the time of his death in 1993, Tuttle had published over 6,000 books on Asian culture, history and art—a legacy honored by the Japanese emperor with the "Order of the Sacred Treasure," the highest tribute Japan can bestow upon a non-Japanese.

With a backlist of 1,500 titles, Tuttle Publishing is more active today than at any time in its past—inspired by Charles Tuttle's core mission to publish fine books to span the East and West and provide a greater understanding of each.

Published in 2006 by Tuttle Publishing, an imprint of Periplus Editions (HK) Ltd.

www.tuttlepublishing.com

LCC Card No. 2006900261

ISBN 978-0-8048-3714-9

Distributed by:

North America, Latin America & Europe	Japan	Asia Pacific
Tuttle Publishing	Tuttle Publishing	Berkeley Books Pte. Ltd.
364 Innovation Drive	Yaekari Building, 3rd Floor	61 Tai Seng Avenue, #02-12
North Clarendon,	5-4-12 Osaki	Singapore 534167
VT 05759-9436	Shinagawa-ku	Tel: (65) 6280-1330
Tel: 1 (802) 773-8930	Tokyo 141 0032	Fax: (65) 6280-6290
Fax: 1 (802) 773-6993	Tel: (81) 3 5437-0171	inquiries@periplus.com.sg
info@tuttlepublishing.com	Fax: (81) 3 5437-0755	www.periplus.com
www.tuttlepublishing.com	sales@tuttle.co.jp	
	www.tuttle.co.jp	

First Edition
15 14 13   12 11 10 9 8 7 6   1305CP

Designed by Daniel Urban
Printed in Singapore

CONTENTS

INTRODUCTION

A Champion's Soul with a Winner's Heart

S O YOU WOULD LIKE to become a champion. Following the advice of actor Robert De Niro . . . "fuhgeddaboutit." It's not possible; it doesn't happen. Having said that, I know I now have your attention. You see, a champion is never something you become . . . ever. It starts now by acting as a champion, committing yourself to practicing the habits and ways of a champion, choosing to engage in a lifestyle that demonstrates such qualities and characteristics on a consistent, daily basis. This "way of being" is, in the words of scholar Joseph Campbell, a "hero's journey"—an up-and-down, gain-and-loss odyssey of self-discovery as you become dedicated to exploring the unlimited boundaries of your full human potential, in athletics and life. Along this journey the true champion must ask: Does this journey have heart, passion, and love? If not, misery and failure will result. If so, success will be the by-product.

Champions are valiant fighters and brave warriors. In ancient times, warriors were courageous, focused, visionary, modest, passionate, and completely selfless, working for the higher good of the group or tribe. They were "athletes" of indomitable spirit and iron will who, by believing in themselves, knew that all was possible. These Zen warriors were specialists in defeating an opponent when the true battle had less to do with external events than with

the battles raging inside themselves. They were fierce competitors who waged war against their inner fears, frustration, fatigue, and self-doubt, and the rewards for such victory were deeply personal and satisfying. Winning was always the by-product of their victories within.

Although certain physical strengths are needed to excel in athletics, there are additional "ways" and qualities that separate the champions from the near champions, a host of internal, intangible characteristics that I refer to as the "stuff of champions." One person who exemplifies these traits is distance runner Keith Foreman, who was told by a world-renowned college coach that he didn't have the "right stuff" to compete at that level—that he essentially didn't measure up. With championlike qualities of courage, fortitude, determination, and perseverance, Keith went on to become an all-American and only the fifth U.S. runner to break the four-minute-mile barrier. In my mind, Keith possessed the Way of the Champion . . . his heart and soul were in it. Keith truly was the quintessential warrior.

As with Keith's experience, a Swiss aerodynamicist once demonstrated by calculations that bumblebees cannot fly. Yet, although the bee has none of the "right stuff" for flight, it seems to be a champion aviator. Like this creature, we all have within us untapped strengths and powers that—once accessed and coupled with proper training and coaching—can enable us to "fly" in our arena of choice.

Yet another example is the legendary racehorse Seabiscuit, considered by the so-called experts to lack star capability. He had none of the traditional earmarks of the truly great horses, yet he ran with heart and became a successful champion. As an interesting sidelight, it is understood in the race-horse culture that only champion horses receive a formal burial ceremony when they die. The heart and head are buried, while the body is discarded, because those intimately associated with the animal know that it became a champion by demonstrating courage (from the French word *coeur*, meaning heart), tenacity, fearlessness, and the willingness to suffer pain—all qualities of a true warrior. Among people as well, the heart and the head make the champion.

Following a close victory against the University of Notre Dame for his team's fifteenth NCAA soccer championship, Anson Dorrance, head coach of the University of North Carolina Tarheels, said, "You win these games with heart, and we spend four years working that muscle." Singer-songwriter

Michael Bolton reminds us of this: "To look beyond the glory is the hardest part, for a champion's strength is measured by heart."

And let's remember that participating in athletics is not a prerequisite for entering into the champion's domain. In fact, most who adhere to the lifestyle of a champion choose other arenas of performance in which to demonstrate these qualities. For example, my wife, Jan, is a true champion in all aspects of her life. I can never forget her dedication, sacrifice, courage, patience, perseverance, fortitude, determination, and bravery during the birth of our children. I thought the grueling pain I experienced during an all-out race, such as a marathon, was remarkable—until I witnessed her courageous efforts during child delivery. Her preparation and training for those events were not unlike the focus of all great champions. Her championlike core continues to carry over to her work as a physician, a runner, and a mother of four vibrant, challenging, active children. Like all champions, she strives to gain positive results, yet savors the process. Her life exemplifies what I call "The Way of the Champion."

This way of champions in athletics and other arenas of life demands high self-esteem, self-awareness, integrity, and the ability to take the risks to improve while using failure as a teacher on the road to self-discovery. While average athletes and achievers are aware of everything when they think they should be, the champion is aware of all things at all times. Champions focus on consistent preparation and performance, and they know that all outcomes and results are natural by-products of strong commitment to a thorough, intense work ethic. In the words of the philosopher Aristotle, "We are what we consistently commit to doing." Champions believe in themselves and display a strong desire to do whatever it takes to get it done. They fail, yet unlike the nonchampion, they tolerate such setbacks as natural, inevitable results of entering the competitive arena—in sports and in all walks of life. They are tenacious, fearless, audacious, proud, and confident in their ability to be this way, win or lose. Of course, they want to win on the scoreboard or get that contract in business, and will do all that is necessary to gain that victory. Yet, they know that such a win or outcome is never certain, and if it comes, it is usually the result of their inner victories. Champions distinguish themselves from all others in that they are willing to sacrifice, suffer, and do everything that the nonchampions will not do.

Champions see sports and life as a forum where they can use their opponents as partners. The word "competitor" is taken from a Latin root meaning to "seek together." When a worthy opponent goes all out, in the heat of a competitive situation or event, you learn to dig deep and discover reserves you never knew existed. Your opponent gives you the distinct opportunity to learn valuable lessons in a condensed period of time. This personal wisdom about winning, and understanding what you are

made of, will enable you to live like a champion in the games of athletics and life. How you meet challenges in sports determines how you approach obstacles in your personal life.

Champions fully grasp the difference between what they can and can't control in an event or life situation, and choose to focus on the former. Outcomes and results cannot be controlled; because of this, one becomes tentative, tense, anxious, and stressed. There are some elements of competition you can control, however, such as preparation, attitude, emotions, work rate, effort, and certain "little things" (see "Little Is Large" in Chapter 9), and these help you to relax, stay calm, and focus with intent. Knowing you can control these aspects of your game builds confidence, and as we know, a confident, calm attitude helps you to perform consistently at higher levels. It's important to realize, though, that even if you control all these aspects of performance, there is no guarantee that the outcome or results will be in your favor; they will, however, enable you to be at your best and feel great satisfaction in the process. Winning, for the champion, is therefore defined as the ability to demonstrate your best on a more consistent basis, by being victorious over those inner demons previously mentioned. Winning, for the champion, becomes a multidimensional experience of winning within, demonstrating personal greatness, and hopefully, achieving favorable outcomes as well.

Thinking about winning in this way takes practice. You do it by means of subtle shifts of the heart and mind. This book, *The Way of the Champion: Sacred Lessons for Mental Strength, Leadership, and Winning in Athletics and Life*, will train you to become skillful in this regard. To help with these shifts, I use the two thousand-year-old Chinese classic *The Art of War*, by the strategist Sun-Tzu, as well as wisdom from other ancient Taoist books such as the *I Ching* and the *Tao Te Ching*. These books offer principles for mental strength, conscious leadership, and strategic winning, for a more fulfilling, satisfying experience than that of the traditional external victory. Such principles, especially for winning, have been used by martial artists, great warriors, coaches, generals, and successful corporate CEOs worldwide. These are universal ways, or the way things naturally work . . . the *Tao* . . . using strategy, tactical positioning, competitive advantage, and self-awareness based on the laws of nature. I have successfully applied Sun-Tzu's and other Taoist wisdom throughout my career with athletes and people in many fields of endeavor. What most begin to realize when using this Tao, or paradigm shift, is how clear and natural the opportunity for inner growth and self-improvement becomes, while they discover personal and collective greatness. Here is a way to navigate the journey of infinite potential. The true champion has all of the foregoing virtues as well as what I call the "Winner's Heart."

It is important to understand that there are many recognized champions in athletics and professional circles who do not acknowledge the Way of the Champion, philosophically. And by the same token, there are many who live the way outlined within this book yet have never been outwardly recognized as champions. The difference between the two seems to be that by living the Way of the Champion, you are assured that you will discover how great you can be . . . that you are capable of reaching extraordinary levels of personal best performance. And, in the process of such performance, you increase the likelihood of being on the podium as well. This "way" is a choice, and you have the power to choose to be a champion or to be ordinary.

I know about this way because I have worked with thousands of national and world-class warrior champions in the NBA, NFL, PGA, and Olympics, as well as CEOs in business and others in all arenas of life. During the last seventeen years, I have published eight books on the Tao and performance, while working with some of the greatest collegiate athletes and teams at Duke, Stanford, Maryland, Missouri, Colorado, Iowa, Ohio State,

Columbia, California, and many others. During this time, I have worked with thirty-eight teams who have gone to a Final Four, with eighteen winning national championships. I have learned more from this experience than I have taught.

In addition to this, I have experienced personal victories in numerous competitive sports, including baseball, basketball, track, cross-country, cycling, distance running, tennis, and racquetball. As a coach, a national-class athlete, sports psychologist, teacher, author, and father of several athletic children, I find that the Way of the Champion is present in my life everywhere.

If you wish to take your game to the next level, what I have learned will help you to discover the greatness that lies within you. What I know is that the making of a champion is all about heart. While the champion sees the game as a battlefield against an opponent or clock, it's also an arena for the battle within, against such demons as fear, fatigue, frustration, failure, and self-doubt. These inner battles are fought with weapons of the heart, or what I like to call "the stuff of champions," the right stuff. In this sense, being a champion is a spiritual practice of embracing and connecting to the right stuff, sacred virtues such as courage, fortitude, compassion, commitment, patience, perseverance, passion, integrity, responsibility, respect, and self-sacrfice. By learning and applying the right stuff, and absorbing the lessons of champions and the wisdom of Tao, you will live your life with the substance and spirit of a champion and be a true winner in every aspect of the game of life.

The Way of the Champion presents clear, concise, natural, and practical time-honored sacred lessons on how to act like a champion. For example, the personal battle of completing an enormous work project, preparing a meal for twenty-five people, or finishing a twenty-six-mile race can seem overwhelming. At mile twenty of a marathon, I have felt, "I can't go on; it hurts too much." This feeling is so intense for many runners that the thought of going six more miles seems problematic at best. However, by going only one more mile, and then repeating that achievement five more times, one learns the ancient lesson: When you divide a seemingly insurmountable task into small, manageable segments, you can achieve a goal. How do you swallow an elephant? One bite at a time.

This Tao lesson, once grasped, is easily applied to all of life's struggles and can enable you to accomplish extraordinary things in any field of endeavor. Tao lessons, through sports, will help you to witness so much of life in small dramatic ways. Andrew Cooper's book *Playing in the Zone* tells us that "sport is a container where passions are channeled and virtues cultivated." Sport is a spiritual event that can enrich the soul, awakening in all of us a higher sense of self, the true winner within.

This book offers a deeply spiritual, unique, creative, inner approach to mental strength, leadership, and winning that will help to steep your mind and heart in a serene, tranquil, and heightened state of self-confidence. It emphasizes a process of thought as well as trust in your intuitive self—a process that basically conforms to the Zen precept of "doing the right thing." You will learn how to reach personal and team best performances by clearing barriers and neutralizing the impact of obstacles standing in the way of success, whether these obstacles come from within, are environmentally induced, or derive from other athletes, teams, or personal relationships affecting you in everyday life. According to Sun-Tzu, best performances are achieved not just by knowing all the right moves, but as much by knowing what not to do and when not to do it.

HOW TO GET THE MOST FROM THIS BOOK

Sun-Tzu's ancient treatise on victory, *The Art of War*, classifies winning into four major categories: Self-Awareness, Strategic Positioning, Competitive Advantage, and Leadership with Team Unity. You will notice that I divide *The Way of the*

Champion into four similar parts. As you reach each major part, my partner, mentor, and friend, Chungliang Al Huang, will greet you with a piece of his beautiful, meditative brush-stroke artwork, capturing the essence and message of that specific section. This will immediately be followed by a relevant quote from Sun-Tzu or other Taoist wisdom, which will set the tone for the chapters within that particular section. Each of the four major parts are subdivided into three chapters, each one filled with pragmatic lessons containing strategies, tactics, quotes, stories, anecdotes, and relevant gems taken from my years of experience with athletes and others, to help you to transform competition, confrontation, and conflict into true art. As a side note, this structure resembles the four seasons and twelve months of the calendar year. In Chinese culture, the cycle of the four seasons represents a complete experience, marking lasting change in habits and relationships. Give yourself this year to create change and establish new habits and relationships in sport and life. When the year is up, begin to read this book again for continued comfort and support in the journey.

At the conclusion of each of the twelve chapters, you will be given a summary of the major lessons to be learned, in the form of usable, practical affirmations. These "touchstones" can be placed individually on 3 x 5 index cards to be referred to throughout the day or week, as gentle reminders and directives to help you stay the course. You can choose all or only those that jump off the page and hit you right

between the eyes. All of my clients use this method to help them stay on track, consulting the cards in various situations, such as during the changeover on the tennis court, between hole and tee box on the golf course, at halftime during a basketball game, just prior to a competitive sky dive, while waiting in the start house before a downhill race, or simply waiting for a bus, plane, or train. You can also use these affirmations prior to an important business meeting, before talking to your children after they have misbehaved, and to help you to make changes in unproductive personal or behavior patterns or daily habits.

Following these statements, each chapter will give you two or more questions, the answers to which will guide and direct you forward on the quest in a proactive, integrative way. These "Questions on the Quest" are meditative, reflective, and soul-searching in nature, helping you to access the deeper, more spiritual aspects of yourself and your journey. Like the affirmations, the answers to these penetrating queries can be written on 3 x 5 cards and used as indicators of what must be done in order to keep on track.

I intend that these chapter-ending exercises serve as appetizers for the athletic soul and personal spirit, helping you to expand your lens of perception by focusing on possibilities, on becoming not the best, but the best you can be. By doing so, you come alive and experience more joy, freedom, and profundity in athletics and life. You begin to perform at a higher level and become more successful in all your arenas of performance.

Having said all of this, I strongly advise against reading the book from cover to cover, quickly. I want you to scan the table of contents and see what topics speak to you. Go to that section and slowly "work it." Digest the morsels, try the exercises, answer the questions, adopt or adapt an affirmation when it fits. Most of us have busy lives, and being on the go makes it difficult to read a whole book. When I read a book of this type, I want to get to the point, learn, close the book, and practice. You may be like this as well. Whether you are a busy athlete, corporate worker, or home manager, I know you can find the time to read the book in this way—perhaps five or ten minutes before bed each day. Give it time during the day to sink in. Little by little, inch by inch, it will be absorbed entirely.

By nurturing and practicing the ways of the champion on a consistent basis, you will develop good habits and increase the chances of performing at more satisfying levels in your life. By being familiar with and entrenched in this way of a champion, by acting-as-if and using these attitudes, precepts,

virtues, and lessons, you automatically place yourself in position to realize your potential.

I'm ready . . . are you? If so, let's begin the journey,
take in the "stuff of champions," and find out how
you can perform and succeed like highly effective
athletes, professionals, workers, parents, and people
who win in sports and life. This book will come
through in the clutch every time, to help you experience more joy, satisfaction, and freedom in any game
you decide to play.

1

THE WAY OF SELF-AWARENESS

When you know both yourself as well as your competitors, you are never in danger. Know yourself but not others and you have half a chance of winning. Knowing neither puts you in a position to lose.

✳ Sun-Tzu

T HE ADAGE "knowledge is power" couldn't be more appropriate for the opening section of this book. It is absolutely necessary to have self-knowledge and an understanding of others prior to entering any arena of competition. The champions are aware of their own strengths and weaknesses as well as those of their opponents. They know their source of motivation and inspiration; they know their true purpose with a clear vision of their direction; they know the tasks and processes demanded of them in order to realize their very best performance. With such awareness, they are in position for sustained success in athletics and life. The following chapters will teach you lessons about how champions gain a more complete picture of self and opponent, in order to position themselves for victory on and off the court.

1. Lessons on Self-Knowledge

> *Surround self with the right people in healthy environ-*
> *ments. This will take courage, compassion, strength,*
> *determination, desire, and a self-created vision for you*
> *and your aspirations. No need to tell others about your*
> *intent . . . just make a plan and carry it out.*
> ✳ Sun-Tzu

ELF-KNOWLEDGE is the true secret, powerful weapon of the champion. Knowing
the court, your plan of action, and your
competitors is necessary, but this needs to
be accompanied by self-knowledge—an accurate
appraisal of who you are and of your levels of physical, mental, spiritual, and emotional fitness. The
champion has the courage to take an accurate
inventory of personal struggles, blockages, obstacles, and fears, and to determine where the most
work is needed in order to go beyond these limitations. Also, knowing your true self is a hedge
against selling yourself short and giving your opponent more credit than necessary. You don't want to
give your competitors permission to make you feel
inferior. Refuse to compromise your talents, toughness, strengths, and courage; play every moment by
demonstrating who you are and what you do have
as a competitor, and feel proud of that. Play with

absolute integrity. Trust this inner knowing and use it; when you don't, fear and uncertainty set in. Do not compromise this integrity; remember that you are good enough and that you deserve to be the best you can be. Regardless of any other competitor, remember that you have value, something very big to contribute, and begin to display all of your attributes as an athlete. This knowledge comes from knowing who you are. The following lessons will help you to identify and expand upon the traits that define you, and help you to begin to consistently perform with utmost integrity.

SELF-ACCEPTANCE

IT ALL STARTS HERE. The champion displays wisdom by recognizing shortcomings and weaknesses, acknowledging and accepting them openly. This is the purest form of self-respect. True champions know that it is perfectly natural to have faults and self-doubt; they accept the whole package yet work to create change and move beyond such limitations. I am reminded that many trees are knotted and deformed, yet live a long, happy life because they are useless to the house builder.

What I notice about all performers, and athletes in particular, is that their relationship to the game in the field, court, arena, or boardroom is a perfect mirror or reflection of their relationship with themselves. When they accept who they are and do what's necessary to improve their shortcomings, they seem to perform consistently at their best levels. Most problems that arise with performers are directly related to their inability or unwillingness to accept and love themselves as they are. If you don't accept yourself, if you deny or fight who you are, the chances of change or growth are greatly diminished. When you accept and love yourself, you are more inclined to do those things that will enhance your performance in athletics as well as daily life.

I have learned from champions that self-acceptance means developing positive self-images and self-talk, images and words that clearly define your strengths and create a vision of what is possible. It requires that you work on the obstacles by replacing them with patterns and behaviors that facilitate your development as an athlete or a person. When your relationship with yourself works, your athletic and personal life will work.

A terrific athlete came to me and said, "I don't want to do it, but coaches are telling me to lift weights three times a week to get strong." I replied, "Don't lift weights to get strong . . . you'll quit. Lift weights to invest in yourself and your team. Do it because you love yourself, then you will be successful." Apply this reasoning to eating well or avoiding things that destroy your body, such as alcohol or drugs. If you love yourself, you will be less self-destructive. Self-acceptance and self-love will make change possible. You will stop putting energy into excusing your shortcomings; instead, you will acknowledge them and move ahead. Say to yourself repeatedly, "I accept all of who I am and consciously choose ways to change what I can and leave what I can't alone." Then use the following parts of this chapter to help you make the necessary shifts.

WRITING MY OWN STORY

THE LESSON to be learned from champions is to ignore all external stories about you, your performance, your abilities, and your attitudes. Champions write their own stories and proceed to do all those things that make those stories true.

I first learned about this concept while working with the University of Maryland's women's lacrosse team. We had won six consecutive national championships, and the media and our opponents were telling stories like: "It's time for someone else; they can't possibly do it again; they aren't as strong this year; they lost to team A, and we beat team A, so we should beat them." Stories from others are created in order to drum up excitement and suspense. Papers and magazines need stories in order to sell. To shift their consciousness to a higher plane, I told these athletes that champions do, indeed, write their own stories and then begin to live them. On the way to the Final Four national championship weekend, I asked each athlete to write a two-paragraph, hundred-word story by completing the following: "The national champion women's lacrosse team from the University of Maryland arrived at the scene of the 2001 championship, staged at Johns Hopkins, and . . . (fill in the rest with strong, positive, affirmative statements that validate your greatness)."

When all of the athletes completed their assignment, we went around our team circle, as each athlete read her story to the rest of the team. The stories were nothing short of phenomenal. The well-chosen words inspired each athlete to show up with intensity, courage, fearlessness, and a willingness to demonstrate how good we were to the entire world of lacrosse. Our focus was on us rather than on all the hype and misdirected comments and energy from others. The team's performance on the field mirrored their creative, heart-centered stories as they scored an overtime victory for their seventh consecutive national championship.

Now, you are not Maryland lacrosse, but I have learned from these champions that there are many negative stories that we all carry around, based on messages from our environment as well as those originating from within. When your stories are negative and counterproductive to your purpose and mission in sports or life, dispel them by writing a story that nurtures, validates, and encourages positive forward movement on your journey of being a champion. You do this by writing about yourself, for the next six to twelve months, weaving truthful, positive, strong qualities into your dream scenario, athletically and personally. For example, start by answering the questions: What are the tangibles I bring to the team, arena, work environment, or home? What are the intangibles? The answers will give you a clue about yourself. Next, think about goals, and write as if the goals have been achieved. You can even take the recurrent negative stories and change them around to reflect more of who you are and what you desire. Whatever story you write, begin in this way: "I, (place your name here), am on a champion's journey from now to (date). While on this path, I attend to my total self—body, mind, and spirit—in the following ways: (then go into some detail of what you do specifically on a daily basis and list what you achieve athletically and personally as well)." Having done this, now affirm some of the positive virtues and qualities you possess that make all this possible. Say, for example, "I can accomplish all this because I am a (fill in qualities) athletic person." Use words that fit or could fit with a little work, such as: courageous, conscientious, committed, fearless, persistent, brave, and tenacious (see next lesson: "Self-Definition").

Once the story is complete—about one page in length—post it in places where you can read it daily. Put it on an index card and read it while waiting for a train, plane, bus, or a friend who is late. Your life is a reflection of the stories you tell. Be a good storyteller.

SELF-DEFINITION

MOST OF US sell ourselves short. When you are asked to choose words that describe you, your choices probably reflect a diminished and unaware self. Out of fear of being labeled conceited, egotistical, or self-centered, most people opt for playing it safe. The truth is always more upbeat and positive than that initial evaluation.

Barbara Israel, a client of mine, is a talented, intelligent author, businesswoman, and aspiring golf athlete. I asked her to choose five or more words that she'd like others to use when describing her a year from then. Barbara chose "lighthearted, clever, charismatic, industrious, and determined," among others. These are terrific qualities, yet they were somewhat conservative. In fact, these words described who she is already, so no stretch there. I told her that she is much more, and that I wanted her to explore the possibilities. So I changed the question. I suggested, "Think of people you admire, particularly athletes, and list the qualities and virtues you most admire in them and would like to develop in yourself. These could be people you intimately know, or some you simply hear about because of their fame or stature in their sport or profession." Using Annika Sorenstam, arguably the best female golfer, and her personal teacher, John, as models, Barbara identified "aggressive, calm, relentless, controlled, detached, and prepared" as adjectives she'd like others to use in talking about her a year later. I told her that when you identify qualities in others that you like yet seem to lack, those traits are actually part of your nature, and they remain dormant unless developed. Capitalizing on this psychology of self, I then asked the most important question: "What five or six actions or behaviors can you demonstrate on a daily basis that would allow others to really see you in this way?" When she listed these, I asked her to do two things. First, write a strong affirmation on an index card, for example: "I am an aggressive, relentless, yet calm athlete." Or, "When I am controlled, detached, and prepared, I play my best golf." Second, on another card, list the actions and behaviors needed to demonstrate those traits, and check each day to see if she did accomplish these tasks. This is an exercise in self-accountability and responsibility, one that reinforces, validates, and directs one's journey as a champion. Now, you can do the same thing. Know that a host of deeper, more meaningful qualities reside within you; they just need to be discovered and practiced. Before long, others will think you've changed, but you are simply manifesting what is already you, your basic core. You must, however, be sure to "work" these words on a consistent daily basis. After three weeks, the change will be apparent. Barbara has followed this way, and changes are evident in her game. People were remarking about her shift after only one week. She teaches us the value of self-definition for higher levels of play. Learn that so much more lies beneath the surface; practice developing these traits.

SELF-TALK AND IMAGERY

IN HIS REVEALING and riveting book, *My Losing Season*, author and one-time national-class basketball athlete, Pat Conroy, states, "We must learn to not listen to the malignant sounds of negativity." This noise can come from others in our lives as well as from the inner voice developed from society's messages. Such self-talk deeply influences self-esteem and the way we perceive or see ourselves— that is, self-image. I have learned this from champions: No matter how good you feel about yourself, the malignant sounds will penetrate your nervous system and dictate the road you travel, unless they are short-circuited by strong, positive opposing messages. Champions know this and take specific steps to stay on track when negative self-talk and images make their entry into their minds and hearts. They do this, not by forcing the negative self-talk and images away, but by substituting workable, upbeat words and phrases, called "affirmations," along with images that support these words.

> *You should exercise unrelenting discipline over your thought patterns. Cultivate only productive attitudes. . . . You are the product of everything you put into your body and mind.*
>
> ✳ *I Ching*

In 1989, while working with the University of California Santa Cruz men's tennis team, the athletes and I came up with the affirmation "Straight Line in '89" to keep us on track. We won the national championship that year, and these words kept these champions focused every day along the way. Affirmations are short statements that are true or have the potential to be true in the future. They direct you toward your goals, actions, and behaviors by reminding you to do those things that place you in position for personal best performances, regardless of the outcome. UCSC may have lost that championship, even though they used this affirmation, but because of it, they did stay focused on doing the right things to maximize their chances. Affirmations are self-direction, not self-deception. They bring you closer to your desires than you would be without them. Take those words that define you, from the previous section, and form your own affirmation. In sports and all of life, remember: The words you use create your reality. Keep them positive and they will provide the power to transform the quality of your existence.

The words you create need to be positive and in the present tense, as if what you are saying is true now; keep them concise and optimistic. For example: "Calm and confident, I play well." "I expect success, I am one of the best." (Success, of course, means the process—executing the plan, as opposed to success on the scoreboard.) "I have all that it takes; I am good enough." Once you write your affirmations, do what champions do. Place each one on an individual index card; carry these cards with you when you travel, and read them several times daily. When you do, imagine that the feeling these words create in you, or the situation they describe, is actually true. For example, close your eyes, take a deep breath, and imagine these words to be true: "I am a strong, vibrant, healthy athlete." Notice the feeling you get. Compare this with "I am a weak, out-of-shape, help-less person." Your nervous system knows and feels the difference.

Throughout this book, you will be given affirmations that will help you to better absorb the concepts to be learned in the chapters. Practice them and feel free to create your own, using any of the lessons within these pages. In his book *Human Options*, Norman Cousins strongly suggests that the principal language of this age "must be concerned with the awakening of vast multitudes to the possibilities rather than the limitations of life."

PERSONAL INSPIRATION

INSPIRATION IS ONE of those intangibles that most of us crave, but very few are able to access when needed. Coaches may shout "Get inspired!" or "Play inspired!" yet nothing seems to happen without some touchstone or reference point.

First off, it's important to know that, by definition, inspiration refers to any stimulus that causes creative thought or action. Being inspired requires a prompting from something written or said, or the presence of a particular person or object, each of which gives life or courage in the heat of performance. Being inspired helps you to become more animated and motivated to carry out a desired task.

Champions often inspire themselves with a simple act of consciousness. They may think about a song, a poem, a passage from a book—like the Bible, Koran, or *I Ching*—a friend, a parent, a character in a movie, or even someone they do not know but have heard about, such as the Dalai Lama. You can do the same by taking words, thoughts, or ideas and pasting them on your locker door or carrying them in your training bag. If it's a person, a picture will suffice. Among some athletes, the use of a well-placed tattoo seems to be a source of inspiration.

When you are out on the court or field, in the locker room or boardroom, getting ready to give a presentation to a large audience or simply on the sidelines, and you feel the need to get charged and emotionally engaged, recite the words, sing the lines, or picture the face and message of the person you admire, and devote your efforts to your inspiration of choice.

Personally, I am inspired by an eighty-four-year-old man who continues to improve his performance in the Iron Man Triathlon in Hawaii. I am inspired by Van Morrison and his soulful voice and lyrics. I am inspired by all the champion athletes who continue to teach me the lessons of diligence, dedication, and devotion to a cause. I am inspired by nature's awesome gift of beauty as I mountain bike high in the Sierras on a balmy summer morning. Who or what inspires you, and how do you access this for future performance?

DEDICATION TO A LIFESTYLE

ALL DEDICATED ATHLETES and other people get inspired, but not all inspired athletes or others become dedicated. Being dedicated is "staying the course" amid the storms of uncertainty. It's not about discipline or motivation. Some people are inspired for a few minutes or days, motivated for a few days or months, yet dedicated for a lifetime. Dedication is the devotion to a certain way, in this case the lifestyle of a champion, in order to make the most out of oneself, to discover just how darn good you can be. Dedication is a deeper, stronger, more passionate level of commitment. Being dedicated is that spiritual space that embraces failures, fatigue, setbacks, mistakes, frustrations, suffering, and sacrifices on the journey of being the best you can be. It requires fundamental faith, trust, and confidence in the process, as you display patience and perseverance while hoping that today you will be touched by the gods. This dedication does not have a schedule, as you never know when a break-through will occur; it could be the next game or the next year. Dedicated athletes and others do not measure progress by how far or how fast; instead, they are more concerned about the direction that their feet are pointed. Being dedicated (or devoted, for that matter) means a certain willingness to do all that is required to grow and improve—even if you sometimes don't feel like doing it.

A modern-day retired champion athlete who demonstrates the virtue of dedication and devotion is Cal Ripken Jr., two-time American League MVP as an all-star shortstop for the Baltimore Orioles. He is the world record holder for consecutive games played, at 2,632. He was dedicated to doing all he could to show up and help his team. Derek Jeter of the Yankees is similar in his devotion to the team. Tim Duncan of the San Antonio Spurs basketball team is another model of dedication.

Champions, I have noticed, know that they are constantly being tested for their levels of commitment and dedication. They understand that the sky is the limit, and they demonstrate neverending devotion and commitment to what they deeply desire and want to achieve. Commitment is the major ingredient that separates those who break on through to the other side and experience personal greatness from those who don't. True commitment is devotion to a cause, ideal, or goal that may be more crucial to you than whether you live or die. To test the level of your dedication and commitment, ask: "What three things am I willing to do in practice (at work, in the home) each day, to prove to myself that I am serious about my commitment to the team, to the office, to the family, and to my own personal improvement?" I ask teams to do this, record the results with each player's name, and pass them around so everyone can see what teammates are doing. We draw up contracts, sign them, and use them for personal accountability and responsibility.

Until one is committed, there is hesitancy, the chance to draw back . . . there is one elementary truth, the ignorance of which kills countless ideas and splendid plans: that the moment one commits, then providence moves too. All sorts of things occur to help one that never would have occurred . . . incidents, meetings, and material assistance which no one could have dreamed would come [his/her] way. . . . Begin it now.

✳ Goethe

Amid all this talk about dedication, you do not want to overlook the "fun factor." It's easy to become way too serious. Stay in touch with the process of winning like a champion. Continue to build a bedrock of love for your sport, your profession, and self-discovery. Champions love what they do, and fun—perhaps defined as the execution of a well-thought-out plan, or simply doing the "little things"—is an essential component of it all.

BEING PERFECTLY IMPERFECT

IN THE WORDS of Carl Jung, "Perfection belongs to the gods; the most that we can hope for is excellence." As we know it, perfection is unattainable. If I waited to write until I had the absolutely perfect words, you wouldn't be reading this now.

Having said this, I notice that many of us still seek

the impossible—the perfect performance—and become frustrated and feel like failures as we fall short every time. We attempt to force what can't be.

What champions have taught me is that perfec-

tion is a standard to go towards rather than a way to measure your self-worth. The goal for you as a champion is to establish what perfection is in a certain situation, and then see how closely you can mimic that result, knowing that if you shoot for the sun and miss, you will still be one of the stars. Champions, I have learned, will refuse to self-destruct when perfection is not attained. They are aligned with the wisdom of the Tao, which asks us to let go of such futile striving. *The Tao Te Ching*, the ancient book of the Way, suggests that we strive for excellence, knowing that failure, setbacks, and errors are an inevitable part of the process of the champion's way. In fact, needing to be perfect causes stress, anxiety, and tension, all of which contribute to being far less than perfect. In more serious cases, athletes who think they should be perfect, yet aren't, resort to drugs, dropping out, and in some instances, suicide as a way out.

The lesson for all of us is simply BALANCE. The champion embraces the delicate balance between the healthy pursuit of excellence—striving for certain standards, with an interest in results—and the outcome. The process involves searching for internal rewards based on flexible, realistic goals.

Emphasize how the game is played, not just end results. Although you may occasionally feel disappointed in the results, never internalize them as a commentary on who you are.

Studies with Olympic athletes have shown that those with balance, those who pursue excellence, have better chances of success than those who set unrealistic, perfectionist goals. I notice this to be true in all aspects of the corporate structure, family life, and any spiritual/emotional endeavor.

Without balance, you are denied the opportunity to risk, grow, change, and live a life of optimal potential. You will be controlled by fear if you attempt to control an uncontrollable world, the world of perfection.

Accept life as a roller coaster, filled with ups and downs, victories and defeats. You cannot be competent at all times. Set goals of perfection, but know they are only guides to help you realize your very best. Joe Montana, Lance Armstrong, Barry Bonds, Gandhi, and Jesus were never perfect. You are in good company. Be perfectly imperfect if you must.

LESSONS AS AFFIRMATIONS

* My athletic and personal life work best when I demonstrate self-acceptance.
* I write my story then do all that is needed to make it true. My entire life is a mere reflection of the stories I tell myself.
* I define myself with strong, positive words, describing

traits I want to develop; then I do what's needed daily to make these words become me.

* My game and life are a reflection of the words and images I choose.
* Affirmations are self-direction, not self-deception.
* Inspiration is a personal act. I think of what inspires me and use it.
* Dedication is the willingness to do all that is necessary to grow and improve as an athlete and person.
* Once I commit to being a champion, things go my way.
* Perfection is something to go toward, not achieve.
* The object is to get as close as I can, and not measure self-worth by outcome.
* I choose BALANCE, the healthy pursuit of excellence, instead.

QUESTIONS ON THE QUEST:

* Having completed all of the questions in the lessons throughout this chapter, you now have a better sense of self. Based on this data, who are you, and where are you going or headed?
* What three things can you do right now that would bring more balance to your game or life?
* Why can you be what you want to be?
* What are the obstacles? What can be done to overcome these?
* What are you most proud of as an athlete, manager, CEO, parent?
* What one book, song, or person has inspired you the most, and in what way?

2. Lessons on Purpose and Vision

*Know your purpose, vision, mission and the message you
want to send and how you will send it. Prior analysis
brings victory; little or no analysis is foretelling defeat.*
✳ Sun-Tzu

WITH A STRONG SENSE of self and
knowing who you are, you are now
capable of developing a definitive
purpose and clear vision for your
journey. This purpose and vision for the champion
is something much bigger than self or any other
individual. In this sense, both are a higher calling
to discovering ultimate greatness. Champions have
taught us that we can take charge, to influence and
control purpose, vision, and mission. In his book,
The Art of War, Sun-Tzu reinforces the athletes'
message when he tells us to take control of environments and be sure to evaluate thoroughly the direction you intend to take. Does it give you what you
need? Are you getting what you deserve? Are all
bases covered? When you make the move, do not
burn bridges behind you. Make sure your destination is a safe one.

In this chapter, you will learn lessons about
regrets, mission, raising the bar, winning, detachment, and more. And one thing is absolutely certain: If you are wondering where you are going

(purpose and vision), you will never get there. Champions are strongly proactive about the journey; they have purpose and vision.

PERSONAL MISSION STATEMENT

MY PURPOSE and vision for writing this book begin with a simple mission statement: to guide and mentor you on your journey to being the absolute best you can be in athletics and life, using the lessons learned from champions. Having stated that, my purpose and vision are crystal-clear as I embark upon this project's path to completion.

So it is with you, whether you are building a career in sport, building a house, or building a family. Being a champion, you need to begin with a simple, definitive mission statement before you take the first step on your long journey. As an athlete, you might consider, as your mission, to be the best you can be. From here, your purpose is to find out from the experts all the things you need to know and do to make this happen. Then you create the images and vision of yourself accomplishing goals and feeling what it might be like to achieve your full potential. This could be a national championship, an all-American, an age-group winner in your sport, a great parent, or a terrific architect and builder of homes.

From a simple mission statement, you learn how to plan the work, then work the plan. Schools and universities do this all the time. For example, most institutions of higher learning have as their mission to educate students intellectually, physically, emotionally, and spiritually. Knowing this, they can begin to develop a curriculum that will attempt to fulfill the mission.

For you, be a champion now by zeroing in on your mission in sports and/or life at this point in time. Start by filling in the statement: "In my sport/life, I am on a mission to _____." The blank is filled in with a specific higher type of goal. For example, you wouldn't say you are on a mission to win the national championship or write a book. That may be a good vision, but your mission, or specific goal, is to find ways to be the best you can be, like lift weights three times a week or write two pages every day. From this, the championship or book becomes a more plausible reality.

There's a fine line between missions, goals, and visions, but try to remember this: A mission statement is an umbrella concept, a simple statement that subsumes numerous goals and tasks. Your mission should help you to formulate goals to identify tasks that, when accomplished, should fulfill the mission. Mission statements are your foundations that help you build castles in the sky. For example, from working with the University of California Santa Cruz men's soccer program, I know that their mission is to use soccer to guide and foster the physical, emotional, and spiritual development of the players. Although winning games is not the foundational emphasis of his program, the head coach, my friend Paul Holocher, is confident that this approach will produce wins as a natural byproduct of the actualization of the mission. From their mission, they have developed a moral code to live by and a plan to elevate their game of soccer. After only six years, Paul's team was ranked third in the nation, playing in the NCAA Championship game, in what was supposed to be a rebuilding year. All this was the result of following their strong, meaningful mission statement.

SENDING YOUR MESSAGE

ALL ATHLETES, upon entering the arena of competition, send a clear, distinct message to their opponents. Champions are aware of this, while most others are not. In fact, when you enter any arena, others will pick up on your message, and what they see will usually determine the way they respond, how they play, and what they do; as a result, your message will impact the results of that event. Knowing this, champions do all they can to control this message, making sure they send one that works for, not against, them. I have had athletes tell me that they will look in the opponents' eyes, and what they see determines the outcome. It has been said, as you may know, that the eyes are the windows to the soul. Athletes have been known to see fear, confidence, tentativeness, intimidation, calm, and other performance-related traits in others. If this is so—and my experience working with champions tells me it is—then what are you doing to make sure you send your best message, whether in sport, at work, or at home?

Let me give you an example that relates to my professional work as a keynote speaker. Before I enter the "arena," I decide what message I wish to send. I want them to know that I am caring, concerned, passionate, and enthusiastic about my reasons for being there. Once I am aware of this, I decide what it will take—what I need to do—to get that message across. For example, I need to make eye contact, move about the room, be energetic, be connected with and "feel" my material, be myself, be sincere yet funny, and be sure to display natural emotions arising from the situations at hand. When I do all of this, the audience receives the message and appreciates my approach. The outcome is determined before I walk out on stage.

Here is an exercise that Sun-Tzu would find useful, given his words in the opening quote about "prior analysis." Before you enter your next arena of performance—a field, court, boardroom, office, classroom, or home—empower yourself by asking and answering these questions:

1. What message do you want to send? The message can be about what they can expect from this contest—that you are a handful to contend with—or it can be that you are in charge, on top of things, ready to go all-out, or simply something like, "I care" or "I'm good."

2. Having done that, what four things, strategies, actions, or behaviors do you need to do that will assure you that your message is both sent and received? Put these into affirmations on 3 x 5 index cards by writing: "When I _____, I demonstrate my seriousness about sending the message." Carry them with you and recite them often prior to the event. Feel the calm and confidence as a result of taking charge.

RAISING THE BAR

CHAMPIONS NEVER ASK whether or not it's possible to raise the bar on their performance, and neither should you. The question they ask is: How is it possible; what do I need to do? So should you.

Know, however, that to discover the possibilities that are available, you must absolutely move out of your comfort zone. Be prepared, as a champion like Lance Armstrong would be, to suffer and sacrifice along the way. Raising the bar in any aspect of your sport, business, or family life demands that you take on adversity in order to experience great expansion, joy, and fulfillment. We tend to be creatures of comfort, and we easily become smitten with who we are and what we've achieved. Still, it is widely accepted that most athletes rarely achieve more than 18 percent of their full human potential.

To raise the bar on who and where you are, and to get a sense of purpose and vision (individual or team), follow the lessons of champions that remind you to focus away from results and more on the process. Focusing on results creates anxiety, stress, and a good deal of tension. Focusing on the process allows you to relax and feel confident in what you can do. To help you to better focus on the process, follow these steps:

1. What are three specific things you could do that you aren't doing now, which if done, would definitely contribute to personal (or team) improvement immediately? For example, in basketball, sprint your lanes, dive on the 50/50 ball, and crash the boards. In life, maybe it's meditate each day, exercise for thirty minutes four times per week, and drink eight glasses of water daily. You decide.

2. Write out a contract with yourself: "I commit to (fill in blank) in order to raise the

bar as a performer in sport and life." Sign it, and be sure to read it every day or prior to entering the arena of performance.

3. Take a few minutes, after you have read your contract, to relax by taking three or four deep breaths, then visualize yourself performing these tasks. Feel the feeling you get when you do good things like this.

Think about how you want to raise the bar in other arenas of life, and follow the same format. It works; it's simple, yet it requires attention to detail.

ZERO REGRETS

WHEN I WORK with champions, they remind me that having regrets is not an option. While it is impossible to eliminate all regrets from your life, the champions teach that regrets can be monitored and greatly reduced or controlled. Over the years, I have developed a method that I have used with hundreds of athletes to help them gain greater control over these demons. The exercise is called "Zero Regrets" and can be used for any path, be it athletic, professional, or personal. This exercise, once again, asks that your focus be more on the process or the journey than the destination.

1. Imagine that it is now six months (or any other significant time frame) down the road, and you are looking back on your season, your work, your fitness program. Using your past experience as a guide, what five regrets could you have at that time? Some say: not giving it my all, not seeing the signs of failure, not being consistent, not lifting weights, not running, not eating healthily, disregarding mental training, and so on.

2. Once your list is created, answer this: What five or more actions or behaviors could I perform that, if successful, would eliminate the chances of having those regrets? These are specific, tangible tasks to be performed, such as: lift weights three times a week for two hours a session, to prevent the regret of being weak in the upper body.

3. Having stated these tasks, take those you are certain to commit to, and begin to create a daily and/or weekly schedule of activity that will guide you to consistent effort.

I have used this exercise with teams when they go to a big tournament or final four. I ask them to imagine it's over, it's Monday morning, and to list the regrets that they could have at that time. Then I ask them to commit to certain activities, tasks, or behaviors that will help eliminate the regrets. This is a powerful refocusing tool usable in many of life's circumstances. Next time you are about to go on vacation, go through the steps and discover how much more fun you will have if you avoid regrets in advance. This will give you a deeper sense of purpose and vision.

OBSESSION WITH WINNING

CHAMPIONS TEACH US that when your sole purpose and vision in sport is about winning, you generally come up short. I alluded to the meaning of winning in the introduction to this book, yet feel a need to elaborate upon it here in lessons on purpose and vision.

I remember clearly the 2002 Winter Olympic Games in Salt Lake City, when Michelle Kwan seemed obsessed about winning gold in ice skating. Having failed to accomplish the feat four years before, she must have felt enormous pressure to win, and she was the overwhelming favorite. However, young Sarah Hughes, who simply showed up to skate her best, having little or no chance to win, skated brilliantly to a gold medal. Her purpose and vision was to skate well, have fun, and enjoy the experience . . . perhaps even have a top-three finish.

When one's only purpose is to win, the tightness, tension, and anxiety seem to build up, hampering one's best efforts. An old Zen saying teaches us: "When the archer shoots for the love of shooting, he has all the skill; when he shoots for gold, he goes blind."

In his classic work, *The Zen of Running*, Fred Rohé eloquently states, "There are no victories except the joy you are living while dancing your run, you are not running for some future reward—the real reward is now!" The modern Olympic games motto, *The goal is not to win, but to take part*, tells us that the essence of participating is not conquering but competing well. By so doing, you embrace victory as a path without a destination, and, as stated by Cervantes' Don Quixote, the journey is better than the inn.

Can you remember a time when you were a winner, even if the results didn't acknowledge it? I finished 143rd out of 310 runners at the Stanford Invitational cross-country race. By most participants' standards, this was not considered a winning performance. For me, however, it was a major victory because I ran my fastest time for the distance and did it against some of the best collegiate athletes in the United States—all of whom were twenty or more years younger than I. It was an inner, personal triumph, one most could not see. When the process itself is fulfilling and you win in the moment, victory is always the experience; external results are ephemeral, while internal victories last a lifetime.

We are a society obsessed with winning. This obsession has led us to forget about the important inner values and virtues of partaking in the activity. Although winning is important for many reasons, it should not be an end in itself. If you believe "you don't win silver, you lose gold," you will create layers of tension, anxiety, and stress that will contribute unfavorably to the outcome. When stressed about the outcomes, your body is unable to move with the fluidity or flow that's so necessary for a winning performance. But as you probably know, even confirmed champions can perform like non-champions. It's easy to get distracted from the important reasons for competing and get off track, but the true champion finds the way back. Olympian and world champion Regina Jacobs is able to find her way back by using an affirmation prior to her 1500-meter races. To relax and focus on the process, Regina reminds herself: "I may or may not win, but I am a world champion and choose to run like one." She takes a few minutes before the race to motivate herself, visualize her performance, and feel relaxed, smooth, and strong as she chooses to compete like a champion.

Think about this: When one eye is on winning or outcomes, there's only one left to focus on the moment. Tell yourself this truth: Your greatest triumphs are always the byproducts of your ability to demonstrate the level you have attained in anything you do. You do this by focusing on the moment, the experience itself, rather than by trying to control the outcome or results.

Finally, it's important to know that in your performance preparation, it's not only okay, it's healthy to visualize winning (against the clock, against an opponent, or for a certain place in the finish), but not to the exclusion of seeing the process unfold as it should. However, when you actually show up at the event, do so to simply perform your best for that day. Remember that wanting to win and needing to win are very different attitudes toward competing. The former is healthy, the latter is destructive.

Now, take four deep breaths, and, in a relaxed state with eyes closed, visualize the following:

✳ Imagine pushing yourself to performing the best you can.

✳ Feel the confidence from performing as you know you can.

✳ Sense the moment-to-moment thrill and excellence.

✳ Experience the fun as you execute your well-defined plan.

❋ Feel the joy, the dance, and the flow of a great performance.

DETACHMENT AND JOY

WHAT DISCUSSION on purpose and vision is complete without talking about the Zen and Tao notion of detachment, accompanied by the joy and fun of participation? The truth is, when we all started out as little boys and girls in sports and life, outcomes had little meaning, and simply being involved was the greatest joy. Many of us as adults lose touch with these concepts and forget that the real purpose of participation is to experience joy and fun. And by "fun," I mean those situations during practice, at a game, or at the office when I feel elated from the execution of a well-thought-out plan, as opposed to a "fooling around" kind of fun, which has its place. But certainly, champions do have fun and keep their perspective by detaching themselves from outcomes or results. If you are not attached to happiness, you usually can achieve it. Detaching from possessions is a freeing sensation. Janis Joplin told us that "Freedom's just another word for nothing left to lose." Our greatest successes are usually the byproducts of our most joyful processes. We seem to be much more effective when we open ourselves to the extraordinary power of detachment. Champions have taught me that, although it's fun to achieve, the greatest joy is to find meaning in the experience of achieving.

I am not suggesting that you detach from results completely. Consider simply detaching your ego from results, whether in victory or defeat. For example, do all the right little things to put yourself in position to win, yet do not measure your self-worth based on negative outcomes and results. On the flip side, do not inflate your self-worth when victorious. You win or lose . . . but you are not a winner or loser. I love to win, champions love to win. Yet once the outcomes arrive, I must feel good in victory or learn in defeat and go on. I refuse to wear a button that claims I am either a winner or loser. The Chinese calligraphic symbol for detachment tells us to cart off old skins and emerge free from physical and mental confinement. Do not let attachments to outcomes diminish your strength or temporarily bolster your ego; you need not become a victim of circumstances. Great champions know that both winning and losing are, as products, ephemeral. The process, how you compete and work the plan, is lifelong. They achieve happiness in this way.

LESSONS AS AFFIRMATIONS

✳   With my mission statement, I plan my path to greatness.
✳   Before I enter an arena of performance, I become

clear about the message I want to send, and do what it takes to make sure it is received.

* I am not afraid to go beyond my comfort zone to raise the bar.

* Adversity and suffering help me to experience self-growth and joy.
* I am aware of potential regrets and do all I can to prevent their occurrence.
* I may or may not win, but I compete and act like a champion.
* The greatest victories are those you achieve in the process of competing well.
* I love to win yet refuse to measure my worth by an outcome or result.
* Winning and losing are short-lived. The experience of playing lasts a lifetime.

QUESTIONS ON THE QUEST:

* What things do you love the best about your life as an athlete, a professional, a home manager, a parent?
* What percentage of your time do you experience these satisfactions?
* How can you increase this percentage? What can be done?
* What specific things would help you to live more joyfully and feel joyful and productive more often at work, at home, and on the court?

3. Lessons on Knowing Your Opponent

Prior to challenging another team or individual, study them; get to know them. Inform yourself about all aspects of the opponents' environment. Base your strategies on awareness and gathered information, regardless of the time or cost involved. Consult with others who have competed against this opponent. Know about your opponent's desire, hopes, and aspirations. This information must work together with your intuitive sense of what's best for the group.

✳ Sun-Tzu

THERE IS ONE THING that all champions agree upon with regard to their opponents: KNOW THEM PRIOR TO ENGAGING IN BATTLE. How much you need to know is not clear and will vary depending upon the situation, the sport, and the people involved. For example, knowing everything about your opponent in individual sports like golf or bowling is not essential. For games like basketball, lacrosse, soccer, and other quick-paced sports, more information may serve you well. How much one gathers often relates to various personality characteristics. Some coaches and athletes are compulsive about knowing all that's available, while others take the essential minimum information and focus more of their energy and time on their own preparation. There really is not a right or wrong. Roy Williams, head basketball coach of the University of North Carolina, may want his athletes to have extensive knowledge about every opponent. Meanwhile, John Wooden, retired UCLA head basketball coach, wasn't as concerned about being totally informed about every nuance of the opponent, choosing instead to put more time into his team and what they could do to raise their bar. Both are successful coaches, both with a different approach to seeking information about an opponent. For you, decide what's best for your comfort level. Acting like a champion, you want to know what to expect and then gear your preparation accordingly. The less surprise the better. And, remember to gather material on the arena or venue where you will be competing or performing. As a competitive distance runner, I made a point of driving the course a day before the race and running parts of it that seemed challenging, particularly the hills. I would even run the last mile and cross what was to be the finish line. Even to this day, if I am performing in an auditorium, giving a talk, or presenting a clinic, I make sure to take in the ambiance a day prior to the event, if possible. I rehearse my presentation with that information in mind. This information relaxes and calms me; I feel comfortable from having been there previously. Champions use prior knowledge about opponent and venue in this same way.

GATHERING OPPONENTS' SECRETS

SUN-TZU, in *The Art of War*, devotes an entire chapter to espionage, the use of well-planned spy tactics to gather the secrets of the opponent. In athletics, we refer to this tactic as scouting the opponent. Everyone does it; coaches and athletes watch an opponent play and record information that could help in their game plan. Teams in conference play may actually trade game videos. When Maryland is about to play Virginia in lacrosse, the coach may secure from Duke the tapes of the game they played against Virginia a week before. It's not always this cordial, yet I find this sharing to be more commonplace.

Gathering opponents' or competitors' secrets is ongoing in everyday life as well. The Thai restaurant sends a manager across the street to have lunch at the Chinese restaurant, in order to discover their secrets of success. He comes back with the big secret—free tea, soup, and dessert included as part of a "lunch special." The following week, changes are made and business picks up at their eatery. Knowledge is, indeed, power, as I mentioned in the introduction to Part I, "The Way of Self-Awareness."

Whether competing in a race, playing tennis with your neighbor, or looking for a winning recipe from a chef, if you want to improve your chances for victory, you need to obtain information. The question "What is your secret?" will help to shed light on this. Collect this data and use it to your advantage. Always ask, if you don't already know, so that your awareness will expand and performance will follow suit.

COUNTERINTELLIGENCE

IN *The Art of War,* Sun-Tzu talks about counterintelligence as the judicious placing of strategic misinformation into the hands of your opponent. Basically, as a coach or athlete, this means that you find a way to enable your opponent's spy or scout to pick up erroneous information that seems to "leak out" of the inner, sacred circle of your team. The strategy is to let them know you in this incorrect way. No need to drive the message home; you simply must be subtle about how you do this. For example, an athlete gets injured in a game and the word gets out that she won't be playing for a while. You make sure that your opponent knows this, because this "leak" could impact their preparation and strategy and give them a false hope going into their contest against you. Come game time on Saturday, your athlete shows up ready to play, much to the chagrin and consternation of your opponent. They begin to feel anxious and confused, which works to your advantage. The truth is, your athlete was not that badly injured, and you let others believe otherwise.

Counterintelligence is the creation of an "appear-ance versus reality" situation. You want your enemy, opponent, or competition to focus on what appears to be true, when in reality, it is not so. The impor-tant point is to make sure the misinformation gets into the hands of those who will deliver the message to the right people at the right time. This takes finesse. I will go into more detail about this in Chapter 4, "Lessons on Deception."

THE OPPONENT WITHIN

You may "know" yourself, but are you aware of the possibility that your greatest opponent could be you? As the comic strip character Pogo once said: "We have met the enemy and he is us."

There is no question about it . . . I am my own worst opponent. My beliefs, self-imposed limita-tions, distorted visions, and negative expressions provide enough obstacles and barriers to stop an army dead in its tracks. They impede my confidence and fuel self-doubt. Sometimes I have felt that I wouldn't want to be part of any team that would have me as a player, to paraphrase comedian Groucho Marx.

Champions have the ability to recognize and identify this inner opponent. They know that phrases such as "I'm no good," "I don't deserve to be here," "I'll never win," "I can't," "It's never been done," "I'm not big enough, fast enough," "I don't have the right stuff," and others like these are in opposition to the direction they desire to go. These phrases become formidable opponents that help to

marinate your nervous system in the juices of negativity, defeat, fear, and frustration. When you begin to recognize this opponent, you can take the steps to defeat these demons with phrases and words that contain weapons of the heart: courage, compassion, patience, kindness, persistence, desire, mindfulness, and tenacity, to name but a few. As with any opponent, there is no need to destroy or kill it. Simply acknowledge these unreliable thoughts, and replace them with words that speak the truth—that is, positive, affirmative expressions that support and nurture your journey.

Do not make a mountain out of a molehill, or make a molehill out of a mountain. The truth is, your enemy within is only a group of thoughts; it is not you. Choose your thoughts well, and react quickly when you recognize the opponent. Sun-Tzu's advice to all of us is "when taking on inner demons be swift, seek out direct, fast routes that keep you going forward . . . don't look back. Prune gently as you are not trying to destroy your whole self." Yes, don't look back; refuse to analyze the garbage in the "in box" and give it validity. Prune a tree too much and it will die. Just trim the branches. Remember that the opponent within suffocates in the presence of positive, affirmative words of truth. This is the Way of the Champion.

LESSONS AS AFFIRMATIONS

✳ I take the time prior to any event to learn all I can about the arena, venue, and competition involved.

✳ "What is your secret?" is a question I love to ask my opponent.

✳ It's perfectly okay for my opponent to receive misinformation about me or my team.

✳ I am fully aware that I may be my worst enemy and take the necessary steps to defeat this demon.

✳ Thoughts are only thoughts; they are not me.

QUESTIONS ON THE QUEST:

✳ In what specific ways do you block your own progress in athletics or life?

✳ What five things can you do right now that would unclog that blockage and help you become a good partner to yourself?

THE WAY OF STRATEGIC POSITIONING

Those who win one hundred victories in one hundred conflicts do not have supreme skill. Those who have supreme skill use strategic positioning to win over others without even coming to conflict. Establish strategies that cannot be defeated.

✳ Sun-Tzu

IN *The Art of War*, Sun-Tzu suggests that the road to victory in competition is the skillful positioning of you and/or your team for triumph over your opponent for defeat. Such strategic positioning can be established prior to or during an event. He reminds us that timing is crucial as you seize the momentum and watch closely the movement of the opponent, as such actions provide the clue to victory. The following three chapters present lessons that you can use to establish a strong strategic position for competition. You will learn the art of deception, how to stabilize your emotional states, and ways to be accountable to yourself and those around you. By learning these lessons, you will, according to Sun-Tzu, "establish a situation that cannot be defeated and miss no opportunity to defeat an opponent." Welcome to Part II of *The Way of the Champion*.

4. Lessons on Deception

Appear to your opponent as inept and less competent; be unknown to them. Show what is contrary so no one can tell what you are doing.

✴ *Tao Te Ching*

THE PITCHER THROWS a change up, the kicker fakes a punt, the point guard sends a "no look" pass, and the runner shifts gears. Hank Iba, legendary basketball coach, once claimed that "the essence of the game is deception." The art of deception is a universal strategic tactic used by athletes, coaches, and teams in athletics, by CEOs in industry, by professionals, and even by parents looking for the edge. Sun-Tzu, in *The Art of War*, emphasizes the importance of appearing incompetent. He says that "victory depends on knowing others while being unknown to them. Deception is a delicate art."

Champions teach us that the key to deceiving your opponents is to display behavior contrary to the plan or what truly is. They wish their opponent to think they are weak, not ready to play, yet they know otherwise. Being deceptive is a simple, subtle, yet powerful proactive maneuver.

ILLUSION OF ADVANTAGE

THE FIRST LESSON in deception is giving your opponents the illusion that they are stronger, faster, and more powerful than you; help them to feel they have the advantage. Champions do this by creating the appearance of being vulnerable or confused or fearful. For example, cyclists use such tactics when they slow down as if fatigued, only to surge briskly and discourage their opponents. Kenyan distance runners are great at creating this and other illusions. Some teams "advertise" fake illness or injury of a star player prior to a big game. Your opponents become overconfident and are shocked when they realize you are at full strength. The essence of all games is illusion and surprise. Sun-Tzu reminds you to capture the advantage by concealing your strengths.

Champions create these illusions as they lull their opponent into a desired place by downplaying their strengths and exaggerating their weaknesses. You, too, can project the appearance of fallibility. It's like giving opponents a "gift" they cannot refuse to take, as you remain poised to strike when the time is right.

SURPRISE AS A COUNTER

WHEN COMPETING, you can use the element of surprise by making sure you do nothing to threaten the opponent. This way, the competition does not pay attention to you, which places you in position to implement your strategy. You can also use the competitive event as an aid rather than a barrier to doing what you need to get done.

Sun-Tzu reminds us to keep secret all plans and resources. If others are not aware of your possible position, they need to prepare for an attack from many places; this will dilute their strength. Experimental posturing, showing one defense and using another, will reveal, under analysis, the strengths and weaknesses of others. All of this contributes to the surprise effect.

In sports, the champion develops many surprise tactics, secret weapons unleashed at unexpected times. *The Art of War* teaches you to execute decisive strategies that your opponent can neither detect, analyze, nor anticipate. For example, in basketball, you can use trapping defenses and full-court presses to confuse opponents. Teams can show a "new" offense or defense pattern, like a four-corners stall in basketball, a triple hand-off in football, or a new breaking ball thrown by a pitcher in baseball. As a strategy, surprise is very effective in creating an advantage. It is exciting for those who use it and can be devastating to those who receive it. If you can keep your opponents unaware of your plan, you can increase the chances of victory. Sun-Tzu calls it genius, the ability to surprise opponents with change and variable formations, causing them to constantly adapt—which brings up the subject of another great tactic for positioning: adaptation. In the words of Sun-Tzu, "no position is a good position." Let's see what this means in our next lesson.

NO POSITION IS THE BEST POSITION

THE IMPORTANCE of flexibility and adaptation to change can't be overemphasized for the purpose of good, strategic positioning. The truly great champions are aware of this tactic, which suggests not holding to a fixed plan of attack, but rather changing according to the unfolding of events. When you are too rigid, you can break. Being flexible and adapting to change, on the other hand, keeps you fluid and allows you to adjust and rise above the change. Those who adapt maintain the advantage. We all need to learn how to adapt. Adaptation is learned and grasped when you are given the opportunity to react to changing situations in practice, in games, and other day-to-day situations. In *The Art of War*, Sun-Tzu again reminds us that "when you formulate a plan be sure that it is realistic given your personality. Is it possible? . . . then execute it. If your opponent is much stronger and bigger and powerful, develop a plan that changes the rhythm, the pace of the game, plan, or objective."

So, in this sense, no position is a good position. Champions formulate their plans but don't blindly stay with them—don't hold their position. Adapt and be flexible. Shift your plans and mind-sets when change occurs. For example, a game is changed from a dirt field to turf. Sunny, warm weather turns to cold rain. Sometimes, the championship finals can be changed at the last minute due to TV programming shifts. I have had clients in the Olympics who are ready to perform when expected and then told that the event will run an hour later than anticipated. Without adaptation tools, you could lose the race before it is run. Sun-Tzu reminds us in *The Art of War* to be certain to have an alternative plan if the first doesn't work out. It's a secure feeling to have backup tactics, such as having additional athletes who can step in and step up when others are injured or sick.

It is impossible to anticipate all eventualities. The best way to plan for something unpredictable is to not be afraid to adapt. If you talk about the possibility of unpredictable circumstances, and understand the importance of adjusting to change, you will be better prepared to shift, when change does occur, and you will feel confident about doing so—regardless of the particular change. Then, when an opponent throws up a surprise on the field, in the office, or at home, you can simply remember that this is a time to be adaptive and flexible.

Look at everyday life, and you will immediately see how to apply this lesson. People often talk about "going with the flow." The only certainty is the uncertainty of life. Change will occur. Adaptation to change is a sign of strength. To rigidly adhere to plans or expectations is a setup for stress, anxiety, and misery. The *Tao Te Ching* tells us how "soft is strong." We will talk more about this later in the book, but for now, *the Way of the Champion* teaches us to let go of the need to be right, soften up, choose our battles, and come out on top. Water is soft yet wears away rock. This is the real strength of the champion in all of life. Bend or break . . . your choice.

SOME OTHER NUGGETS

HERE ARE SOME other gems or nuggets from *The Art of War*, used by champions to help strengthen their strategic positioning:

❋ There is no need to destroy your opponent. You can gain the advantage over them by using a chrysanthemum as your sword. If you embarrass your opponent, it could come back to bite you.

❋ Be quiet and swift. Prolonged events put a damper on vigor and vitality. No overtimes, please. Strike to get what you like.

* Study your opponent's style and know when to challenge.

* Attack when you are strong; defend if you are inadequate.

* Keep a low profile, with all attention away from you. Then you can build up your strength while they have no reason to suspect you as a threat. Conceal all strategy, even this one.

* Train yourself to be in position to compete error-free. Turnovers, base on balls, mental lapses, errant passes, interceptions, and double faulting are some of the more common errors and mistakes athletes commit. If you work daily on diminishing such problems, you create a situation that cannot be defeated. By doing so, you secure yourself against attack.

* Never underestimate the strength of your opponent. Always prepare thoroughly. Refrain from being smitten by victory and complacent. Remember David and Goliath. Playing against a weaker opponent requires conscious integrity and tenacity, or you pay the price.

✳ Refuse to pit one athlete against another on the same team. Competitiveness within the same team could be a detriment. It's okay to be "worthy opponents" for each other, but it must be achieved in the spirit of love. Because they love each other, they should go all out and practice at high levels against each other, because by doing so they are helping their friends to be better prepared against other formidable opponents.

✳ Challenge or attack when you are smooth or ready, not when confused or uncertain. (Time-outs are needed in such circumstances.) Attack without using all of your energy. Be the first to establish a strong, advantageous position. If opponents are not as well prepared, be sure to jump all over them immediately (don't give them time to gain any confidence).

✳ You must tune in to your opponents' spirit (inner determination), composure, and strength. Attack when their spirit is down or idle. Also, confront opponents when they seem disorganized, confused, or chaotic. Finally, your opponents' strength is compromised when their familiar, normal routines are disrupted.

❀ It's important to know what your opponents rely upon to function well. What are the attachments? What is needed in order to be victorious? When you discover this, make every attempt to seize it. Get the star to foul out; slow the game down when they are attached to running up and down, back and forth; speed it up if they like it to be slow; play zone if they depend on single coverage.

❀ You gain advantage by seizing opportunities quickly, and especially when unexpected. Attack the weaknesses at all times.

LESSONS AS AFFIRMATIONS

✳ When I display behavior contrary to the expected plan, I put myself in position for victory.
✳ Whenever I can, I give my opponent the illusion that he or she is stronger, faster, and more talented than I.
✳ I downplay my strengths.
✳ My genius is the ability to surprise opponents with change, causing them to constantly adapt.
✳ No position is a good position, if I am flexible and adapt.
✳ I constantly seek ways to become more adaptable.
✳ I go with the flow, like H_2O.
✳ Soft is strong. I let go of the need to be right and I am, therefore, happy.
✳ Quickly strike to get what I like.
✳ I attack when strong and defend if inadequate.

QUESTIONS ON THE QUEST:

✳   In what ways can you use deception strategies that you are not doing now?

✳   With these strategies in mind, what would it be like to compete against you?

✳   Which deception strategies do you notice are being used by your opponents?

5. Lessons on Emotional Management

Competition does not cause anxiety. Any emotional reaction . . . getting supercharged, displaying team emotional spirit excessively . . . is an indulgence that could distract and reduce levels of energy so needed for success. You need to not display "contrived emotions"; it's what teams do when their self-doubt needs an artificial boost. If you know yourself and your opponent . . . objectives and motivations . . . then all the "hoopla" is unnecessary.

✱ Deng Ming-Dao, *Tao Wisdom*

The Art of War identifies unnecessary emotions as fundamental causes of turmoil and defeat. According to Sun-Tzu, those who detach, those who are calm and reserved, prevail over opponents. It is the unemotional who seem to win most often.

In my book *Creative Coaching,* I talk about how athletes create a huge advantage over an opponent when they appear unemotional, calm, and detached, even though fire may rage within. I call this relaxed intensity, and it applies to both coaches and athletes. Becoming outwardly angry, frustrated, or upset (although at times this may not be preventable) is a sure indication of your loss of control and an admission that the opponent is getting in your head. Athletes, particularly in individual sports, begin to walk the path of defeat when they begin to display negative emotions. Expressions of these emotions create an inner instability and distract you from playing your game. Strategically, it's wise to function outside the sphere of unnecessary emotionality. You see this in golf and tennis all the time. An athlete breaks a club or throws a racket, and the opponent smiles (even if only on the inside), knowing that victory is certain. As CEO, head coach, or head of a household, you must notice how your emotions defeat you and act to control them. The following lessons will teach you some of the specific ways that you can address issues of emotional MANAGEMENT, to self-regulate and compete as a champion.

THE EMOTIONAL CONNECTION

WHAT I NOTICE about many athletes is how satisfied they are to go through the motions, to simply exist and do things today exactly the way they did yesterday. Champions, however, desire a deeper connection with their sport.

What I want for you is to experience the difference between really feeling connected out there on the field, or in your daily life, and just existing. Too often, you and I think we are connected to what we do. The typical "game day energy" is shallow, lacks "backbone," and has no base. There needs to be a deeper, more personal emotional energy, or *chi*, in Chinese—one that arouses intensity, excitement, and joy, as opposed to pressure, anxiety, and tension.

Champions can project their chi, and when you learn to do it as well, your performance in athletics or any arena in life will move to a higher level.

It's very simple, yet not necessarily easy. How far you go, how great you become in athletics and life, depends on how strongly you become connected—body, mind, heart—to the situation, the arena, the relationship, the task. Champion athletes are like great actors, who, while on stage (the sports arena), project their deep energy, love, passion, courage, feelings, by "acting as if" they truly are that character (that champion or national-class athlete). It's not their technical skill that makes them stand out, but their *presence*, their ability to connect with true emotion. They are rarely thinking of their lines (their moves, their plays, their equipment as athletes), because that would hinder their ability to play or act. It would interfere with their spontaneity, so crucial for staying connected. The lines (moves, plays in sport) are a natural extension of who you are and how strongly you stay connected to that. Here are some strategies for you to use to project your chi:

❀ Identify specific positive emotions or feelings you could have on the field, on the court, or in a business situation. Connect with these emotions—feel excited, joyful, courageous, brave, relaxed, intense—and then go into the arena and let it happen. Let things unfold as a result of your connection with these feelings.

❀ Get connected beforehand by feeling your love for the game, the reason you play, and the good feelings you derive from "doing your thing."

❀ What do you do and how do you act or behave when you are feeling passionately connected?

All of the championship teams that I have been associated with have this quality of getting connected emotionally to the essence of the game itself, *the moment in a lifetime of moments.* Fans love their teams to display this connection. The real thrill is to observe a group of athletes who display such emotion collectively. It's electric—it's the "show-time" feeling one experiences as part of this phenomenon.

Now, once again, create your vision of how you want to play and of how you want to feel. In a deeply relaxed state, created by taking a series of deep breaths (see next lesson, "The Still Point"), feel the "feeling," the energy, and project it to the game. How does it feel when you are passionately connected? Marinate your nervous system in this energy, in feelings you have had in the past when being successful, and duplicate them now for today's performance. Ask yourself the penetrating question: "What do I really love about my sport?" and use the answer as one way to reconnect to the game.

THE STILL POINT

Carefully train to avoid anxiety during competition. There is need to have a way to gather and harness positive energy and to compete with relaxed intensity, free of fear, able to risk, little or no self doubt and courage to thrust onward.
  ✳ Deng Ming-Dao, *Tao Wisdom*

TO FULFILL THE ADVICE of this Tao wisdom, I help all of my athletes and clients to practice MINDFULNESS, a way or system to help quiet the mind (meditate), calm the body, and marinate the nervous system in positive images and self-talk. The Tao calls this state of mind the *still point*, a place of inner quiet and peace. Champion athletes are trained to find this place, which raises awareness, makes movement effortless, and confidence more robust, while providing emotional care. You should know that Tiger Woods's mom is a Buddhist and taught him how to find this still point through meditation at the age of seven, so the story goes. Phil Jackson, former coach of the world champion Chicago Bulls and L.A. Lakers, has used mindfulness techniques with his athletes to connect the team's mission and goals with everyday realities on the court and in their personal lives.

If you want to find your still point, try the following Westernized meditative steps, a combination of various principles from Zen meditation, yoga breathing, and imagery psychology. Do this with eyes closed, in order to block out unwanted external stimuli:

1. Breathe in slowly through your nostrils, and as you do, feel the coolness of the air coming in as it fills your lungs. Imagine the breath going to all parts of the body.

2. When your lungs are filled to capacity, hold or suspend your breath for five seconds.

3. Slowly exhale through the nostrils, and as you do, feel the warmth of the air as it exits the body.

4. Repeat this process seven or eight times, focusing on the alternating cool/warm temperatures of the breath. Notice how, with each breath, you begin to get more deeply relaxed.

5. In this relaxed state, introduce images of success along with words, phrases, and affirmations that positively nurture, rein-

force, encourage, and support who you are
and what you do and where you desire to go.

6. The whole process takes only seven to ten
   minutes each day.

You can use this tool to help you get more deeply
connected to your emotions (see "The Emotional
Connection") as well as to any vision or scenario
you wish to create in your life. My book *Thinking
Body, Dancing Mind* can take you further with this,
if you are interested. This should be enough to get
you very relaxed and focused on positive directions. I use this breathing exercise quite often when
I want to perform more effectively and efficiently.
For example, I will create this still point just prior
to going on stage to deliver an important keynote
address. It helps me to stay connected to my purpose, my material, my audience, and my very best
self. It works well for any other anxiety-producing
performance situations, such as taking an exam,
your first day at work, or going for a job interview.
   In addition to this technique, you can access this
quiet, productive state by focusing on only those
things in sport and life you can control and letting
go of all that you can't. You can never control outcomes, results, or statistics such as points or goals
scored, hits, pins knocked down, and strokes on the
golf course. If you obsess about trying to control

these, you experience layers of anxiety, self-doubt, stress, distraction, fear, and tightness, which adversely affect how you plan or perform.

Focus, instead, on those things that you can control, such as your stride, your swing, your stroke, your defense, sprinting for a 50-50 ball, boxing out, your intensity, preparation, enthusiasm, attitude, courage, and desire—to name a few. Because it is possible to have confidence in what you can control, you can remain relaxed, fluid, strong, and empowered, thus creating an environment where the still point can flourish.

Joseph Campbell, famous scholar and world-class runner and athlete, has written about how he lost two important races in his career trying to control what he could not, the outcome of the race: "I lost the still place. I put myself out there to win the race instead of to run the race . . . and the whole thing got thrown off."

Working with the University of Maryland's field hockey, basketball, and lacrosse teams has provided me with much insight into this concept. Prior to each game, we talk about this still place. I remind them in the locker room prior to a contest how normal it is to want to go out on the field or court and beat the opponent. I suggest that they simply show up, stay connected to their mission, and demonstrate what great players they are—and the victory will take care of itself. They realize, too, that they may or may not win, but if they keep that still place, they probably will play their best, which, in most cases, is good enough to produce victory on the scoreboard as well.

Here are some specific strategies to help you let go of those things you can't control by focusing on those things that you can:

1. Take it to another level personally by refusing to measure your self-worth by the outcome on the field or in life. Know that you are much more complex and important than a simple game, event, or routine.

2. Rather than trying to win, simply demonstrate your ability to perform up to your capability—nothing more, nothing less.

3. It's healthy to maintain your desire for triumph, but realize that you don't really need it; victory is an illusion of lasting happiness that rarely fulfills its promise.

4. Focus, instead, upon redefining "winning" as the ability to demonstrate more effectively the skills and talents learned during your lifetime.

5. Just do it; perform without care. Dan Jansen, world champion speed skater, finally won

the Olympic gold when he decided not to care so much about winning. Don't be too concerned about doing it right. Enter one event and try to not give a damn; if you do this, you will be better able to relax. Sometimes it's more fun to show up and just say "To hell with it"—"it" being the outcome. Having acknowledged that, proceed to perform with what I call effortless effort, an attitude of asserting your best level of fitness, giving your best effort (showing what you've got) without the conscious attempt to win a game or secure a contract.

I have devoted much time to this topic because I have learned from champions that if you master these concepts, you will perform at higher levels, more consistently, with greater courage and confidence. Confidence is simply that spiritual space where you feel free to focus on only those things you can control (see Chapter 6). When you do, you will be calm and, more often than not, discover that still point within. And yes, use your meditation skills often.

INSTANT POSITIVE RESPONSE

In *The Art of War*, Sun-Tzu reminds us that "whenever a doorway is opened by an opponent, enter with lightning speed so that they can't respond.

Anticipate when this could happen during a contest so that you are prepared." This doorway swings open when your opponent has a blocked shot, a stolen pass, a terrific home-run-saving catch, and many other situations in business or life where you fail to respond in a positive manner to your opponent's good fortune.

Also, this door swings open for you to enter when, throughout a game or event, you experience a personal error, mistake, setback, or failure. It may simply be a frustrating situation like a missed shot or a defensive lapse, in sport, or a poor decision, a missed opportunity, a wrong choice, in life. If you let it immobilize you, you will compound the problem; you do not have the luxury to feel sorry or bad for yourself. When you drop your head, sulk, complain to the official, or throw a tantrum, you demonstrate disrespect to other teammates, your coaches, your coworkers, CEO, wife, or kids. When you fail to respond quickly to these circumstances, you give others a boost in confidence, while your self-absorbed reaction has a deleterious effect on your personal performance in all arenas of competition.

You can reverse this process by simply taking a very deep breath (in sports like tennis, golf, and others that give you time for this) and/or say to yourself: "Get going, NOW!" I train athletes to do this by using their meditation technique to visualize, each day, circumstances that cause negative reactions, and to "feel" themselves responding in positive ways. I call this "I.P.R."—Instant Positive Response. I.P.R. can be the touchstone you, your teammates, and coaches can use to create positive reactions immediately. Begin to use it now, and you will change your negative ways of responding to your opponent's good fortune or to your mistakes, errors, setbacks, and failures. In this way, each situation is an opportunity for a new beginning, to begin again. Miss a shot . . . I.P.R., strike out . . . I.P.R., drop a pass . . . I.P.R., double fault . . . I.P.R., rim the cup . . . I.P.R., bad choice . . . I.P.R., poor decision . . . I.P.R., missed opportunity . . . I.P.R. Get the picture?

BEING COMPLACENT

> *Whenever a battle, confrontation or competition occurs, you must keep vigilant at all times. You must stay in touch with your purpose, who you are and what you are capable of doing. Avoid, in the process, thoughts and words that distract and take you off track. By constantly aligning with your strengths, you gain advantage over the opponent.*
>
> ✳ Sun-Tzu

THE WAY OF THE CHAMPION is a process of keeping in touch with and attending to your purpose and ultimate possibilities; it is about looking for ways to be the very best you can be . . . even if you are already great. Michael Jordan arriving an hour early for practice to improve his game or Tiger Woods on the practice green for two hours after a good round of golf, to strengthen his weak spot that day, are two examples of great champion athletes whose path and purpose are to discover their individual best performance. To be less than their very best, even as great as they are, is to settle, to become complacent. Gandhi once said that "life is a constant vigil." The true life of a champion is a constant daily vigil as well, searching for and practicing those behaviors that contribute to your growth and development, on or off the field.

Complacency is an emotional mind and heart space that requires attention. It is anathema to the Way of the Champion, a cancer of the competitor's soul that can be cured or managed by a commitment of the heart. That is, you must have the conviction or desire in your heart to do all that it takes to discover just how great you can be. Are you willing to do all that it takes to reach your full potential and/or be a champion? If you ask "What will it take?" you are not willing or committed. Think about it. What difference should it make if I tell you what it takes? You are either going to do it all or not.

Many athletes and other performers are extremely complacent. They are smitten with their place in athletics or the business world, good enough to participate at high levels with respect to everyone around them. I see this with scholarship athletes in major Division I programs. They are "good enough." But, are they as good as they can be? Not if they are unwilling to do all it takes to raise the bar on

themselves and enter a new level of personal greatness. To be willing to do all that it takes—deep desire—requires the element of suffering, a Zen concept that tells us how adversity is the doorway to enlightenment, or for performers and achievers, the key to discovering and becoming awake to (aware of) their true greatness. It is through suffering that you connect with your deepest athletic and personal self and have the vision of your ultimate greatness. Most of us do not believe in the element of suffering, and that could be why so few people become champions.

Being surrounded by many champions, in athletics and my personal life, I have learned that all championship levels of performance contain some element of suffering—physically, mentally, emotionally, spiritually, socially. To be unwilling to leave your comfort zone and enter into zones of discomfort is to forever be oblivious to how great you might have become. Athletes (elite ones at that) moan more or less incessantly about their difficulties and burdens, as if their sport were supposed to be easy. I know about this moaning because I have done my share.

Sport, by its very nature, evokes in us frustration, grief, sadness, regret, anger, fear, anxiety, anguish, despair (just like life, but more intensified over a short duration). These are uncomfortable feelings, often as painful as physical pain.

Suffering takes on other aspects as well. Long practices, grueling workouts, less free time to socialize, sitting on the bench, and scheduling sacrifices. When my son Sean was fifteen, he was complaining about having basketball (a sport he loves) practice for three hours on a Saturday. His sport requires sacrifice because there's so much going on in the life of an adolescent on any given weekend . . . sleepovers, surfing, skateboarding, sleeping in . . . all healthy, normal things for him to do, yet none of these helps him to discover his greatness as a point guard. It's really fine to not desire something; you just must know that without the willingness to sacrifice and suffer, you probably will fall short of your potential in that area.

Remember, the cure for complacency in any arena of life is commitment of the heart. I am referring to having a deep desire and willingness to doing all it takes to grow and expand, requiring nothing less than courage, compassion, fearlessness, tenacity, patience, perseverance, and a host of other qualities that enable you to forge ahead through any suffering. When you do, you grow physically, mentally, and spiritually. Through all adversity and pain you learn and blossom. Ben Franklin said, "These things that hurt, instruct."

The choice is either to be content with how great you are among your peers or to discover just how great you could possibly be, regardless of others.

EXCESSIVE EMOTIONALISM

It's not wise to build up hate and anger over an opponent and challenge them for personal reasons. It's a mistake to get personally revengeful. Keep your mission clear and without emotional overlay that could possibly hinder clear vision.

✳ Sun-Tzu

SOMETIMES, coaches and athletes question whether they display enough emotion in practice or games. What I notice is that "getting up" for any performance is really not a question of emotions. A "rah rah" attitude is often just a show of a team's need to convince themselves and others that they're ready. It's a question of being in a state of "relaxed intensity" (from using meditation, visualization, affirmation), a balanced state of mind where you can respond clearly, intuitively, and intelligently to the unexpected, the unknown, and the constant swirl of every changing game condition. Excessive emotionalism, the buildup of hate or anger toward an opponent, while at first it may seem to motivate you, can create an unstable psychological state leading to fatigue, confusion, nervousness, lack of clarity, indecisiveness, and egotism—all inner blockages that are more detrimental than a force inflicted by any opponent. The idea is to free up your natural, spontaneous, outward expression of emotion, the result of the overflow from a full heart. It starts on the inside and bleeds outward, rather than the other way around. The key is to let any outward expression of emotion be the result of the natural passion and intensity you feel about the upcoming event.

After a very intense performance and win in cross-country mountain biking, national champion and Olympian Travis Brown threw up his arms and grinned like a big kid as he crossed the finish line. His emotional display was his release after a tough, challenging race.

LESSONS AS AFFIRMATIONS

* I choose to function outside the sphere of emotional vulnerability, and when I do this, I claim the advantage.
* When I perform, I act as if I am a champion by controlling all that is within my power.
* I project the presence of a champion by being passionately connected to how that feels, and I demonstrate it during a game.
* I use meditation, visualization, and affirmations to relax, focus, and play like a champion.
* I cannot control results, so I focus on controlling the process.
* When I commit an error or make a mistake, I use I.P.R.
* In order to improve, I must sacrifice and suffer, as adversity is the doorway to greatness.
* I refuse to remain complacent. I desire greatness.

QUESTIONS ON THE QUEST:

* In what specific ways might you have to sacrifice and suffer? What is sacrifice and suffering for you?

* What five aspects of your sport, work, or life (physical, mental, emotional) can you control? What needs to be done to take control?

* What two specific situations in your game or life cause you to overreact and get emotionally upset? What, specifically, can be done to help you avoid these reactions or get back on track quickly when thrown off?

6. Lessons on Readiness

*The rule of combat is not to count on opponents not com-
ing, but to have ways to deal with them when they do;
don't think they will not attack, but develop what cannot
be attacked when they do.*

✷ Sun-Tzu

THE THREE MOST IMPORTANT ELEMENTS in the strategic plan of champions are preparation, preparation, and . . . preparation. If you fail to prepare, you prepare to fail. Top-notch champions are thorough, probing, and comprehensive as they ready themselves for the inevitability of attack. No stone is left unturned to build body-mind-spirit preparation. They practice their strengths and strengthen their weaknesses. In *The Art of War*, Sun-Tzu looks upon this as the business of calculation for future victory. In preparing for future confrontation, Sun-Tzu advises that you avoid being too willing to lose, too eager to win, too emotionally involved, and too sentimental; otherwise, you will be too vulnerable and in danger of defeat. Being ready means placing yourself in position to quickly respond, to be flexible, and to adapt to any and all eventualities. The athlete or team that is so prepared will enjoy the fruits of their work. The great champions do this well. The following are some examples of how

champion athletes strategically position themselves and prepare for success.

76 GOING WELL, NEEDS WORK

READINESS, the delicate art of being prepared, is
an ongoing process of learning from setbacks
while using your strengths as springboards for
future success. Once an event, game, or contest is
history, it's time to move forward and prepare for
the next encounter. How well you move forward is
strongly influenced by your evaluation style, your
critique of a practice session or performance in a
game. Most athletes tend to begin with the dark,
gray cloud: What's wrong, and why am I (are we)
falling short of my (our) expectations? I usually
joke with an athlete by saying: If you lower your
expectations (see "Expect Nothing"), you will no
longer have this problem . . . but no need to do that.

The key to using past experience for future success
is to ask yourself or your team some well-directed
questions. It's crucial to begin this evaluation
process on a positive note. First, ask yourself or the
team: "What's going well?" This precludes any
chance for defensiveness, either from you or the
team, and sends the message that you (we) are on
track. Positive observations are always available
and, when discussed, will boost confidence and self-
esteem. Such a beginning helps to keep the heart

open for a discussion on any changes to be made. For the next question, avoid asking "What went wrong?" as this forces you to focus on the negative behaviors or actions. Rather, the question "What needs work?" is a proactive, forward-moving question of growth and improvement, helping and guiding you to a place of readiness. Notice the difference between the responses to each question:

A. What went wrong? We didn't make our foul shots.

B. What needs work? We need to practice pre-shot routines, as well as taking fifty foul shots per day.

The first question leads to moaning, complaining, and a focus on what's not being done. It's a reminder of how much we lack. The second question acknowledges that something positive needs to be done to "kick it up a notch." Following "What went well?" it is easier to take on the challenge of "What needs work?" This is simply the journey of a champion in a nutshell: Notice what works well and improve what can be improved. The latter will keep you going forward in a strong, focused, and deliberate way. Use these two questions in your business on a regular basis, as a way to check in and evaluate the performance of yourself and others. It is a nonthreatening exercise that keeps the ambiance upbeat and open to growth. I use this with my kids at home with regard to their schoolwork or athletic performances. They tend to listen, which is a slight miracle in itself. For myself, at the conclusion of any clinic, workshop, or talk, I find these questions to be a constant source of well-being, validation, and potential growth or change.

EXPECT NOTHING

IN THE WORDS of an ancient samurai warrior: "Expect nothing yet be prepared for anything." Expectations, as we know them, can be our strongest opponent, a nemesis for readiness. They are a setup for anxiety, pressure, and stress. Failure to achieve them can be discouraging if not devastating. Remember reading in an earlier section about letting go of what you can't control? Expectations are uncontrollable entities that distract you from the champion's process of focusing on the execution of a well-thought-out plan.

An integral part of any preparation process is to follow the advice of the samurai warrior. Prepare for the possibility of anything happening, and let go of expecting outcomes and results. Having said that, if you have prepared thoroughly, done what's needed to perform well, and feel you are in good shape, you can have the following expectations, and no more:

* Expect to do your best, even it that doesn't mean winning.

* Expect to do well.

* Expect to have it all come together.

* Expect that something really good is about to take place.

* Expect success, which is defined by your ability to demonstrate your present best level of performance on a consistent basis.

* Expect to get to know yourself and become a better athlete and person.

Make your expectations consistent (congruent) with what you feel is realistic for you—not what the media or others expect.

You may feel strongly that you are going to win, and that's good. However, to expect nothing less than victory is a setup for too much anxiety. Better to focus on how you will compete during the contest or event; expect to be courageous, fearless, happy, intense, patient, bold, daring, if you so choose, and let the outcome take care of itself.

Be aware that the media and other external influences can fill your mind with expectations.

These potential sources of stress can create "stories" that do a disservice to your mind, forcing you to focus on the wrong expectation. This can build layer upon layer of anxiety and tension that distracts from your best performance. (Go back to the section "Writing My Own Story.")

When you put aside expectations, you accept that you can't control your future, only influence it. To help with this, focus on the direction in which your feet are pointed at each moment, and establish a strong preference instead of an expectation. A preference presupposes that you have less concern for the outcome, yet can still direct your efforts along the path of excellent performance. You keep yourself open to possibilities for greater expansion, rather than limit yourself with defined expectations. According to Taoist wisdom:

> *Without expectation,*
> *One will always perceive the subtlety;*
> *And, with expectation,*
> *One will always perceive the boundary.*
> ✳ *Tao Te Ching*

And finally, prepare yourself to be free of outcome expectations by attending to the following thoughts in a relaxed meditative state, a tool you have learned earlier in this book. Try to remember a time in your life when you felt relatively free of the expectations of others. You were the new guy on the block, a neophyte at sport, new on the job, or simply a child who was totally oblivious to the "shoulds" and "musts" of the world. Now, in your state of relaxation, recreate the feelings associated with those days when you were relaxed and free of pressure. Your performances reflected your love of and joy in the game or job. Transfer this feeling to your present situation, filled as it is with others' expectations. Say to yourself, "I refuse to give others permission to control me with their expectations. I am doing what I prefer to do, to satisfy no one but myself. I enjoy the process and continue to focus on the joy I feel now."

INTEGRITY IS THE WAY

THERE IS REALLY ONLY ONE way for a champion to challenge an opponent, and that is with complete integrity. For purposes of this discussion, integrity is defined as the narrowing of any gap that may exist between who you say you are and what you, in fact, do. This is why Part I, "The Way of Self-Awareness," is such a crucial beginning to your journey as a champion. When you take the time to discover your sense of self, you begin to feel your personal power.

The message from the *Tao Te Ching* is clear: Trust in the power within, and use it. Lao-Tzu believed that when we as athletes or people in all competitive arenas do not feel this power, we feel fear. Fear creates tension, anxiety, and stress, which limit performance. The Tao teaches you to become aware of your inner power, who you are, and to stay in touch with it and align your action with it, in order to create excellent performance. Knowing who you are puts you in the best position to act on such inner power. Champions do not compromise their talents, abilities, and sense of self, regardless of whom they play, what the score may be, or the situation they find themselves in at work or at home.

So many teams and athletes do compromise their integrity by knowing who they are but not acting accordingly, or by not really knowing who they are, and, unaware of their power, turning away from their true selves and selling themselves short because of intimidation and fear. They give other teams permission to make them feel inferior, undeserving, or less than they are, and they crumble in the process. Integrity is also compromised when you, as the superior team, find yourself ahead by twenty points, only to let the opponent in the door by not continuing to play with the same intensity. You give your opponent the message that you are not willing to demonstrate your greatness for the entire game, that you hope you can relax and not work. Once this happens, they lose respect for you. You can keep your integrity by teaching them how a great team refuses to play anything less than their best until the "fat lady sings" and the bus is warming up.

> *People often spoil their work at the point*
> *of its completion,*
> *With care at the end as well as the beginning,*
> *No work will be spoiled.*
> *✳ Tao Te Ching*

You are only a champion when you exhibit your integrity throughout, regardless of the results. Whether you're the favorite or the underdog, ahead or behind, you can stay in touch with your integrity by focusing not on the score or possible outcome but on your willingness to exhibit your skills, demonstrate your level of conditioning, and play each and every moment of play.

Remember that you are "good enough." You deserve the best, so act *as if* this were true. Regardless of anyone else's position, you have deep value, something to demonstrate, something to teach. You deserve the opportunity to display your level of ability when it is time. Always act as if you are a champion, and a champion you are.

One of my favorite exercises to do with athletes has evolved from this Tao wisdom. Prior to a huge game, I ask them to define who they are at this point in time. They will often say: "We are determined, courageous, relentless, brave, pesty, fearless, and tough national-class athletes." Then I say: "List five specific behaviors that need to be demonstrated during the game in order to prove these words true about you, that you have integrity—the act of combining who you say you are with what you do." This creates excitement, challenge, focus, confidence, and accountability because we now know what it is that we demand from each other. These words and subsequent behaviors become our guide and mantra for playing with integrity. In the middle of a contest, you can now hear "be brave," and these words become a reference point to that spiritual space of being brave. You actually have specific actions you can take that demonstrate this virtue as you play.

As you can see once again, the code of the champion is based on the attainment of inner success. It is understood that you always want to win. You dream about it and can taste it. Yet, show up to play your best, and let the win take care of itself. The champion knows that once inner success is achieved, there is less need for external victory, because you feel good inside. With less need for external victory, there is less tension, anxiety, and pressure over having to win. And, with less anxiety and tension, it is easier for the relaxed champion to achieve external victory, the byproduct of the successful spiritual journey, the goal you actually strive for.

When you begin to adapt and develop in this way, you will notice an overall decrease in the pressure, tension, and anxiety that accompany all competitive situations. You should still feel the excitement, anticipation, and nervousness of the event, as these feelings will keep you on your toes. As a champion, show up knowing that your training and preparation for the game or event are as complete as they can be for now, and simply perform as you are. Don't obsess about outcomes or results; set your body, mind, and spirit free to do what they do best, what you have trained to do. Free of judgment or criticism, let the mind and spirit dance with what the body already knows how to do from all the hours of practice. Enjoy the dance, the flow, the process, and the real reason why you play or participate in any event, just for the passion you have for this graceful sport or challenging work, the joy and the fun of it all. This is, again, what I call integrity, when you integrate who you are with what you do. If you say you are a champion and do the things champions do, you demonstrate high levels of integrity and will be assured of success.

> *Hold to your ethics and principles and do not for a moment consider compromising what you believe to be right. Acting with integrity is the key.*
> ✳ *I Ching*

THE BEGINNER'S MIND

In his classic bestseller *Zen Mind, Beginner's Mind,* Shunryu Suzuki states: "In the beginner's mind there are many possibilities; in the expert's mind, there are few." We are all in danger of being experts.

In preparation for what lies ahead, many of us develop preconceived biases and beliefs that could seriously impede our performance. Being the expert, you "know" that this or that cannot be done. Breaking the four-minute barrier in the mile run was considered impossible. Yet this limited belief was quickly shattered as champion Roger Bannister, keeping an open mind, did what the experts believed to be impossible.

To better prepare yourself and get ready for your performance, be like a champion and develop the beginner's mind, one that is open, receptive, and nonjudgmental. Question all of your limiting beliefs. John Lilly, a psychologist researching dolphin behavior patterns, said that "beliefs are limits to be examined and transcended." Right now, write out a list of your favorite limiting beliefs, such as "I can't," "It never could happen," "I'm (we're) not good enough," and on and on. Begin to see the ways in which you act like an expert, with no basis for proof. Now, with a beginner's mind, change these statements around (example: "I can. . . ."), and then list ways that demonstrate possibility rather than improbability. A pertinent guiding question that will help you open yourself to such possibility is: If you freed yourself to play up to your capacity, what do you think would be possible?

Prior to any performance, I tell athletes that this could be their day for major breakthroughs. I ask them: "If you freed yourself to play up to capacity, what would that be like?" Then I ask: "What specifically needs to be done to make that come true?" Regardless of what happens, their nervous systems are aligned with openness and receptivity to their greatness. They begin to seek out ways to fulfill the dream. To think the opposite will discourage them and contribute to the demise of greatness.

I like the concept of "new beginnings," which reinforces the Zen mind approach. For example, you are a golf athlete who hits a poor shot. As you approach the ball for the second shot, tell yourself that "here is a new beginning, a chance to start again and demonstrate how a champion, world-class golfer hits a ball." In tennis, each point becomes a new beginning. In soccer, each possession is a new start. Each half in lacrosse is a new game. Come out after halftime and play as if the score is zero-zero, whether you are up or down. After each mistake, error, or failure, begin again. "New beginnings" becomes a theme throughout the entire match or game. Having this as a pre-game strategy is a relaxing way to begin the contest.

Another strategy that will help you to keep the beginner's mind is to play with the question: "What is it like to compete against us or me? How might the opponent feel?" Viewing the competitive event from your opponents' perspective will reinforce what you know about you, and help you to focus on your presence rather than to concentrate or obsess about what you may lack. You become ready to demonstrate who you are and see how others may have serious concerns about competing with you. Give them reasons to justify those concerns by performing with integrity.

The more of a beginner's mind you can develop, the more you will play for the love of playing, like a little child in a sandbox, free of judgment, pressure, and the fear of failure. The more you are in this state of mind, the more you free yourself to play up to your capacity.

LESSONS AS AFFIRMATIONS

*   When I fail to prepare, I prepare to fail.
*   I am better prepared when I am flexible and adaptable.
*   My preparation tells me to expect nothing, be ready for anything.
*   Expect success!
*   Look for specific ways to align who I am with what I do.
*   I refuse to give others permission to make me feel inferior.
*   My beginner's open mind prepares me for my personal best performance.
*   My preconceived biases close my mind to opportunities. I examine these and go beyond.

QUESTIONS ON THE QUEST:

*   Based on your preparation, what five positive things could you expect to happen during your performance? (No outcomes or results, please.)

* What five specific things do you need to do to make these become true?
* When you are at your best, what specific behaviors, actions, or attitudes contribute to it? What can you do to bring these to the event or situation?
* Looking back to the past game, tournament, season, work situation, or family outing, what are you most proud of? What can be done to influence that in the future?

THE WAY OF COMPETITIVE ADVANTAGE

Seize opportunities so that others do not gain. Take paths and attack locations that are unexpected.

＊ Sun-Tzu

THE PRECEDING TWO SECTIONS address the way of self-awareness while knowing your opponent, for the preparation of competition, as well as measures to give you strategic positioning prior to and during the conflict. In Section III, you will be introduced to strategies that can be used during an event to help you gain the competitive edge. In *The Art of War*, we learn that time is of the essence, and quick responses are required; these strategies, therefore, will help you to act on instinct derived from your experience. It's crucial to remember that your opponents' greatest advantage—their competitive edge—is your lack of belief in your ability to perform your very best. This part of the book will help you to become mentally tough and to believe in yourself by focusing on all aspects of the game that can be controlled. As you have already learned, when you become obsessed with outcomes and results—dimensions that cannot be controlled—you experience tension, anxiety, and pressure that lead to self-doubt, loss of confidence, and a lack of belief in yourself. These chapters will help you to gain the competitive edge by learning the lessons and strategies from champions and the wisdom of Sun-Tzu that will empower you to function at deep levels of satisfaction, while improving your chances for victory as well.

7. Lessons on Embracing Adversity

A tree hemmed in by giants
Requires tenacity to survive.
　　　　✴ Deng Ming-Dao, *Tao Wisdom*

A s the quote by author Deng Ming-Dao suggests, without the adverse conditions of being blocked by others, the tree in the forest would not have to gather its strength to grow tall. The adversity, itself, enables the tree to become great, just as all adversity in our lives presents us with the opportunity to discover how great we can be. Fear, in the presence of adversity, exacerbates the problem. Determination, resilience, and perspective will enable you to successfully emerge from the danger by staring fear in the eyes and using it as an advantage.

Adversity is a form of spiritual crisis triggering many emotional responses such as self-doubt, loss of confidence, frustration, panic, pressure, anxiety, and stress. Yet, like all crises, it becomes a gift in disguise. In Chinese, the word "crisis" is made up of two characters: *wei*, meaning "danger" and *chi*, meaning "opportunity." It is both danger and opportunity simultaneously. Translated, it means "opportunity blowing on a dangerous wind." In order to discover this opportunity from adversity or crisis, you must, like the champion, show determination to bounce back as well as demonstrate resilience, the quality of digging deep to find a "second wind." Such mental toughness, coupled with

this philosophical, spiritual perspective, will often reveal the silver lining of the cloud. In adverse scenarios, if you keep your cool, observe, and refrain from harsh judgment and despair, you will hear your inner wisdom and be in position to embrace the opportunities opening to you from each crisis.

Athletics is a perfect environment for learning lessons about how to deal with crisis because, in the space of a one-hour contest, you are forced to face some or all of the many forms of adversity: defeat, mistakes, errors, failure, frustration, fatigue, injury, plateaus, and even success with its fleeting nature. By learning to adjust the focus of your lens of perception on these forms of adversity, and beginning to embrace them for what they ultimately offer, you take your first step on the way of gaining the competitive edge in sport as well as all of life.

PLATEAU POWER

MANY ATHLETES detest reaching a plateau along the way of personal development. They lose patience, become frustrated, and attempt to force something to happen before its time has come. Discouragement leads to desperation, which further complicates an already tenuous situation.

On the other hand, champions teach us the benefits of plateaus both in training and in competition. Rather than perceive plateaus as another block to progress, they accept them as necessary and essential holding patterns on the path of mastery. Champions teach us that such stages are not a danger, but an opportunity to learn, through repetition, how to become adept at this new level of performance. These athletes understand that forward movement occurs when the time is right, not when they think they should advance. You may have performed at a higher level once or twice athletically or professionally, but that doesn't mean that you now have the understanding, development, and maturity to function consistently at that level. Your physical, mental, emotional, and spiritual selves must be equally developed before consistently going to that next level. This takes time, and champions persist with patience while waiting for this to happen. In the world of cycling, there's an expression that relates to this: All is possible . . . it's just time in the saddle.

Getting to be your best demands this time. Love the plateau; it is your friend.

CHALLENGING WORK

CHAMPIONS ARE TOTALLY COMMITTED to developing a strong work ethic. As previously stated in the section on complacency in Chapter 5, champions desire to do all that it takes to accomplish the task. They conduct a needs assessment, plan the work, and proceed to work the plan. In most cases, that which separates the champions from the second tier is that the champions are willing to take on all challenges and do all those unpleasant tasks that the others refuse to do.

Allow me to tell you a story about my competitive days as a distance runner. I would train three to four hours a day, every day, logging 100-plus miles a week. I remember feeling tired, exhausted, and sore both mentally and physically at the end of the day. Yet I totally loved it. Sometimes I would go out on a cold 17-degree January night and run an eight-mile loop on a country road, with a friend driving a car behind me for illumination and safety. I knew that not many were willing to feel this pain—they didn't want success as badly. My work ethic challenged me and placed me in an enviable position. From this, I was able to win a national team title and several individual regional championships. I feel confident that in life I can accomplish whatever I desire because I am willing to work harder and smarter than my competitor.

The lesson to be learned from champions is that all great accomplishments in life require us to pass the test of a strong work ethic. It is not something we are born with; it is learned and developed over long periods of time. Get out of bed before others and go to the gym. Add something to your training program. Arrive at the office before others to get the jump, challenge yourself to write two pages every day. A work ethic takes work to develop. All champions know this and receive much recognition for such a work style. A work ethic is a skill that anyone can learn.

Here is an astounding fact. Many in the know believe that the greatest athletic champions in the world today are neither Olympic champions nor the stars of professional sports, but the "marathon monks" of Japan's sacred Mount Hiei. Over a seven-year training period, these "running buddhas" figuratively circle the globe on foot. During one incredible 100-day stretch, they cover 52.2 miles daily—twice the length of an Olympic marathon. But the prize they seek is not a pot of gold nor a few fleeting moments of glory; rather it is to capture the greatest sense of awareness one could ever achieve: enlightenment in the here and now, which will allow them to become modern-day saints. This is indicative of a group of people's commitment to embracing adversity through a driving work ethic, which symbolizes the determination of a champion who aspires to achieve. Their message to all of us is clear: If you do what seems impossible, there is nothing that cannot be accomplished.

PAIN OF HOLDING BACK

CHARACTERISTIC OF CHAMPIONS is their utmost respect for themselves and their opponents, often manifested by their refusal to hold back. Yet there are times when they lose sight of this concept by not giving their all, thus jeopardizing their integrity and possibly the outcome of the game. For example, the national champion women's field hockey team at the University of Maryland "held back" in a devastating 3–2 loss to conference rival Virginia. The pain following the game was not the loss but the fact that they didn't give their best effort. At a meeting later that week, we discussed how the pain of going all out is nothing compared to the deeper pain of waking up the next morning wondering how great you might have been, if you hadn't held back. That following weekend they stepped up and put it on the line against Old Dominion University. Despite a tough 1–0 defeat, the women felt confident, strong, and satisfied with their champion-like play. Committed to playing this way, during their next outing they went on to beat a very strong North Carolina team. By not holding back, the pain of going all out has its rewards, regardless of the outcomes.

Why hold back in any performance of life? Take on the pain and fatigue and use this all-out effort as a guide to help you measure your growth and develop-

ment as a champion. It's not about the opponent—
ever. It's about you and your own definition and
standard of what is extraordinary. Use your opponent as a partner who, coupled with his or her all-out
efforts, can help you discover how good you truly are.

THE SUCCESS OF FAILURE

WHEN WORKING with some of this nation's
best athletes, I notice they share at least two
common traits. First is a high tolerance for setbacks. They teach us to accept failure as a necessary
experience, the price you pay for taking the risks to
become your best. Second, they make more mistakes than anyone. Mistakes are the result of trying
more. They learn from their mistakes, improve,
then succeed.

Failure and setback are equated with crisis.
Remember that the word for "crisis" in Chinese
means two things simultaneously: danger *and*
opportunity. Champions perceive failures as
opportunities to learn, and then, with their new-
found knowledge, they begin to experience success
and forge ahead. Three-time Olympic gold medal
winner Jackie Joyner-Kersee has held nineteen
world records in various track and field events. She
was not always a winner, but always a champion.
She claims that losing a race, and understanding
why, allowed her to become the resilient champion

she is. In a sense, failure was her success, her best friend in sport.

The following strategy will help you to see your setbacks as success opportunities, and help you regain your perspective in all aspects of sports and life:

1. Record the objective facts about the situation; for example, "I got dropped by the group on the first hill," or "I couldn't complete the workout," or "I couldn't meet the deadline for the proposal."

2. Record your subjective judgment about this experience; for example, "I'm a terrible athlete, worker, person. I don't deserve to be part of this. . . ."

3. Record your feelings in response to this subjective judgment; for example, "I'm disappointed, depressed, and upset."

4. Record the objective data that supports the judgment in Step 2. There probably is no conclusive data to verify your comments.

5. Record what you've learned from the setback; for example, "I need to focus on hill

repeats in my training," or "I need to pace myself at the start of races," or "I need to be more organized and manage my time more effectively."

6. Record how you now feel, based on Step 5. For example, "I'm still disappointed, but I'll be okay. I'm better because of it, and I look forward to another try."

In addition to this strategy, you can continue to strengthen your resilience by embracing failure or setbacks as a positive, natural, inevitable process. After all, there are two types of performers: those who fail and those who will. The following guidelines will help you to use failure to your advantage:

✳ Establish realistic, challenging short-range goals. Since you are likely to achieve these goals frequently, you will build in the psychological message that "I am a winner; I accomplish my goals." This will ignite courage, confidence, motivation, and commitment for the future.

✳ Remember that it is absolutely impossible for anyone to be thoroughly successful, competent, and achieving. Failure is part of the process of success. Performance is a roller

✺ coaster, and to think otherwise is extremely irrational and the cause of much stress. Ups and downs can be expected. You win some, lose some; you're hot, you're not. Don't fight with yourself when failure, the teacher, pays an unexpected visit. Open up to learning from it.

✺ Mastery takes time. Patience, persistence, and perseverance are the three P's of extraordinary performance.

✺ True failure can be defined as your unwillingness to see the positive and take the risks to grow and improve. You never want to look back with regret and wish you had taken the risk to go all-out and find how good you could have been.

✺ Like the Zen warrior, expect nothing, but be ready for anything. Expectations with regard to outcomes are setups for failure. Establish strong visions of preference, and then do everything within your ability and power to bring those preferences to fruition.

✺ Failure is not devastating; you probably won't die from it. But it is disappointing.

When you look back upon outward success or failures in competitive situations, you'll notice that they're rarely indicative of absolute truth: You are never as great as your best victory, nor as bad as your worst defeat. Refuse to give too much credence to your results.

Once you have a handle on this perspective on failure or success, you may want to create affirmations to be used as touchstones to keep you on the right track. Create your own or tailor any of the following to your needs:

❀ Failures are lessons from which I learn and forge ahead.

❀ Adversity leads to inner strength. I am a better athlete, worker, person because of it.

❀ I act, not react; I learn from failure.

❀ Setbacks are my teachers; they help me to go beyond my limits.

Finally, use the tools of meditation and visualization (go back to "The Still Point" in Chapter 5) to guide you to success from failure. In your mind's eye, see yourself correcting the mistakes and errors you made this week, and feel yourself performing exactly as you'd like, having learned from those setbacks. Make the corrections over and over in your mind, until you can feel the exhilaration of doing things correctly.

In the martial art aikido, the fighter blends with an opposing force, moves with it, and uses it to his or her advantage. Try this approach with failure: see it as a gift and an opposing force to blend with, as you use its lessons to your advantage. By so doing, you cause the power of the opposing force (failure) to cease to exist. You redirect the force and forge ahead.

Just as the tumultuous chaos of a thunderstorm brings a nurturing rain that allows life to flourish, so to in human affairs times of advancement are preceded by times of disorder. Success comes to those who can weather the storm.
✳ *I Ching*

I truly enjoy taking the opportunity to inform my athletes about my impeccable, somewhat impressive, three-page résumé. I mention how my apparent professional and athletic successes are real, yet create an illusion of the absence of failure. The truth is, those three pages of successes are the result of three hundred pages of rejection, failure, setbacks, and mistakes, without which I wouldn't be who I am today. Buddhist philosophy would say that the arrow hits the bull's-eye as the result of a hundred misses. My failures are my successes. This perception of setback and failure strengthens my resilience, as I am determined to bounce back wiser and stronger than before. The champion sees that there is no alternative.

Remember to keep this perspective whenever you face any kind of failure. You've realized tremendous physiological, psychological, mental, and spiritual benefits from your diligent efforts; to become tense over a poor performance negates much of what has been gained. Not only are a few failures and setbacks inaccurate indications of your abilities and potential, they may very well be the key to your greatest breakthroughs and successes. I am reminded of the wisdom of Tao: "In the Natural Law some lose and in this way gain." I can tell you this: Today's failure won't matter in ten years, but failing to continue to go forward might.

THE DANGER OF SUCCESS

SUCCESS AND VICTORY on the scoreboard of sports and life present us with another type of adversity: how to handle the inevitability of decline. The Tao teaches that cycles and change are constant. Therefore, when you win an event, you believe that you have "arrived," yet eventually you will experience the "fade." The ancient Chinese book of transformation, the I Ching, reminds us that "the zenith is usually brief. . . . When decline approaches, the superior man does not consciously anticipate it, for he expects such cyclic changes. He is concerned with making the best of matters at hand."

The champion understands that all successful results and outcomes are followed by loss, and all loss is the foundation for future triumph. Champions teach us the importance of enjoying the moments of victory while they last, yet knowing that in decline, they will use their setbacks as building blocks for self-advancement.

Another, more subtle, danger associated with success is how it could potentially threaten other aspects of life: job, family, friends. After all, if you are really good at sports, business, or any other activity, you may be tempted to devote more time to your passion to become even better. This could mean devoting less time to family and friends. Those who succeed can easily experience some pressure not to break away from society's stereotypical expectations, and they could feel a twinge of guilt for achieving beyond conventionally ordained limitations. For example, if you are a thirty-eight-year-old who is experiencing success as a runner, you may feel that you're avoiding responsibilities as a parent, if you devote more and more time to training as an athlete. Others may wonder when you will ever "grow up." Also, success in business may create a problem for friends who see less of you because of work commitments.

And then, unlike its counterpart, "failure," success seems to present little opportunity to learn. It can distort reality as you forget your weaknesses and exaggerate your strengths. Being successful creates the sense that you are the best, the expert who knows all. In truth, there may be much to learn, especially if your victory was against a less talented team or an inferior company. You run the danger of becoming smitten or complacent with your performance, as we discussed in Chapter 5.

The lessons from champions and the wisdom of the Tao are clear: Once you achieve success, you can help yourself ride the wave, without sabotaging it, by seeing your success as part of the larger process of life. Use your success as a feedback mechanism that indicates you are on the right track. Set new goals that will keep you on this path into the future. Remember that real success is the quality of that journey. Understand that cycles of decline are usually followed by cycles of expansion. Accept this balance and all that it has to offer.

THE FATIGUE INTRIGUE

LEARNING THE LESSONS about fatigue is an important step in gaining the competitive advantage. Champions know that fatigue is universal, it spares no one, as it touches all age groups and all levels of ability—not only in sports, but in other arenas of life as well. Acknowledging this truth, the champion can relax, which, in itself, helps to relieve fatigue.

Fighting fatigue is futile; if you resist, it will persist. The effort to combat it will only expend energy, increase anxiety, and exacerbate the uncomfortable situation. Instead of fighting it, cooperate with it. Try to think of it as a familiar aspect of self-discovery. Talk back to it: for example, "Oh, it's you again. You always seem to visit me at this stage of the race or this time of day. Fine, you can come along if you wish, but I'm not slowing down or giving up—so hurry and join me." By conducting such an imaginary conversation, you automatically reduce the anxiety by refusing to grant power to this nuisance.

Fatigue can also be triggered by the mind before the body is actually ready to become tired. How many times have you been running along smoothly in a race when suddenly an unanticipated hill appears, and fatigue mysteriously sets in? Perhaps you have found yourself getting tired after being passed by a runner you know you could beat. Maybe you've been at work for hours, accomplishing a great deal, when suddenly you think about how much more needs to be done, and you begin to experience an energy drop. These situations, where the mind becomes burdened by what lies ahead, create an anxiety response, which can lead to tightness and other negative physiological reactions that contribute to the onset of physical fatigue.

How do most of us respond to fatigue? We lose confidence, become distracted, feel frustrated, negative, and fearful. To combat these reactions to what is inevitable, try the mind-set of the champion, by doing the following:

1. Focus on one small segment at a time. With five miles to go in a marathon, focus on running one mile only, then repeat it four times. At work, chop off fifteen-minute segments at a time. With writing, I may simply try to complete a segment of a chapter rather than complete the whole thing at once.

2. Focus on how close you are to the finish, if that is so.

3. Concentrate on the mechanics of your sport, form, and pace, as well as other task-centered considerations, to distract attention from the discomfort.

4. Know that all the others probably hurt and feel tired at this point in the contest, or during a hard workday. They dislike the fatigue as well and are getting more tense as time goes by. If they can do it, so can you.

5. Focus on relaxing your face muscles. Imagine the tightness in the shoulder dissipating. Let your muscles "hang on the bones."

6. Bargain with your body. Tell it you will get a massage, take a hot bath, and rest as you nourish it with healthy food.

7. Change your view of fatigue. Tell yourself that this is the feeling all champions experience when pushing through to the next level, a necessary feeling in the exploration of your full potential.

You have many alternatives for coping with fatigue. I suggest giving each one a try to see what works best for you. Prior to each event, mentally prepare the strategies you will employ. Knowing that you are in control will stall the anxiety and mitigate fatigue. At the first hint of pain, put your strategies to work. Keep in mind that you can take charge of fatigue; you need not suffer through it.

INJURY AS MEDITATION

INJURY, as with all adversity, presents the champion with a crisis that triggers a myriad of emotional responses, from denial to anger, depression, confusion, and, hopefully, acceptance. As danger blows in, opportunity presents itself in many ways.

First of all, if injury were to talk, it would tell us, "Something is not right!" This is a perfect time to reflect upon and reevaluate what is happening in your life. The I Ching sees this as a natural time to "nurture your body and soul . . . look for wisdom in your acceptance of these times." Such thinking requires a shift in perception. For example, you can view your injury or illness as the body's way of saying "take a break." See it as a period of rest and recuperation from which you will bounce back and reach greater heights. While your legs are "on hold," work the cardiovascular system by swimming, biking, and weight training. Many athletes are pleasantly surprised to find they can achieve a higher level of fitness while injured because they've become more determined to "do it right" and stay injury-free.

Your perception of the injury or illness is crucial to the healing process. Give yourself hope . . . and why not, since most athletic injuries and stress-related illnesses are treatable and eventually heal. A lack of hope creates much tension, depression, and anxiety, which inhibit the path to recovery. This "secondary injury" effect exacerbates the situation exponentially. The use of meditation techniques (as discussed in "The Still Point," in Chapter 5) has proven beneficial with such secondary problems. I help injured athletes and ailing clients by giving to them positive mental images and asking them to feel their bodies being healthy, vibrant, and strong. I tell them to affirm each day, "Every day, in every way, I get stronger and healthier." This instills them with courage and hope, thereby relieving muscle tension, which in turn aids the recovery process. Science is still uncertain just *how* the mind is able to accomplish this, but there is growing evidence in medical literature that it can be done. O. Carl Simonton, M.D., author of *Getting Well Again*, has had incredible success using imagery exercises with cancer patients. His research shows that a high correlation exists between positive treatment results and positive attitudes of patients using visualization in concert with other therapeutic approaches. I strongly encourage athletes to use visualization in much the same way.

Finally, it is crucial to understand the importance of laughter in the treatment of injury. Could it be that your grandparents' adage—"Laughter is the best medicine"—holds true? The great philosopher Kant believed that laughter produced a feeling of health through the furtherance of the vital bodily processes. Freud also found humor to be a useful way of mitigating tension in his patients. Maybe the "laughing Buddha" is an image for all of us to emulate.

Research is now showing that not only laughter, but all positive emotions, especially happiness, cause the brain to secrete endogenous opiates (endorphins) that relieve pain and tension. When you lack a sense of humor and react negatively to life's events, you allow those events to ultimately dictate how you feel and live. You give them permission to make you feel unhappy, irritable, or frustrated.

Brooding will not help heal an injury. Use this time of discomfort to gather emotional strength. Work on freeing yourself of self-pity and resentment about your misfortune. Such a conscious change in attitude will hasten the recovery process.

LESSONS AS AFFIRMATIONS

* All good growth and improvement is accompanied by adversity. With determination, resilience, and perspective, I emerge successfully.
* Adversity is both danger and opportunity. I remain aware of the importance of both.
* I go with the flow on my plateau. Plateaus are important components on my path to mastery.
* All of my accomplishments are the result of a strong work ethic and learning from failure and setbacks.
* The pain of going all-out is much less than the pain of holding back.
* Loss is my teacher. I lose and, in this way, win.
* My successes are the result of learning from my failures.
* Fatigue is part of the journey. Everyone becomes tired.
* I take the necessary steps to control this demon.
* I use injury as a time to meditate and reflect upon possible change and direction in my life.

QUESTIONS ON THE QUEST:

* What five examples of adversity do I need to embrace in my life and athletics?
* What five actions can I take now to better cope with these adverse conditions?
* What possible opportunities could come my way as a result of this adversity?
* What lessons am I supposed to learn from all my adversity?

8. Lessons on Champion Virtues

*In conflict and competition the power of virtue is greater
than the power of weapons.*
✳ Deng Ming-Dao, *Tao Wisdom*

THE CHAMPION'S JOURNEY is not unlike that of the sacred path of the warrior or the Native American vision quest. Such warriors were characterized by inner strength, mental toughness, and independence, and they fought for a higher good, beyond self-interest. They understood, as do champions, that the game is not only fought on the battlefield against an opponent; the game is also an arena for the battles within, against failure, fear, fatigue, frustration, self-doubt, and ego. They chose to fight these battles with "weapons of the heart." These weapons are called virtues—competitive virtues more powerful than traditional weapons themselves. These virtues are compassion, modesty, persistence, courage, yielding, fortitude, belief, sacrifice, and respect.

The word *te* in Chinese means "virtue," as in the *Tao Te Ching*, the classic book of the virtuous way. Being a champion is a spiritual act of practicing these inner virtues of the heart and finding ways to connect and demonstrate them in all arenas of your life. By practicing these virtues and integrating them into your performances and life, you will strengthen your competitive advantage and be a champion person as well.

MODESTY

> *When his [Chinese leader Meng-Chih-fan's] people were routed, he was the last to flee. He said "it was not courage that kept me behind; my horses were slow."*
>
> ✳ Confucius

WHEN YOU COMPETE, there is always that danger of becoming too self-involved, smitten with your prowess or level of play. The opportunity to display your wares, make claims, and boast is readily available. The Code of the Champion states that the more you try to look good in the eyes of others, the further you separate yourself from your integrity; too much egocentric, self-absorbed behavior ultimately creates battles within, leading to diminished confidence, and much self-doubt.

I have learned from champions that if you begin to become aware of and experience such self-absorption, it is time to switch back to a more modest place. Do this by telling yourself that an attitude of unassuming modesty brings greater success over time. By having this attitude, you actually begin to feel less of the pressure and anxiety created by having to live up to great expectations, and as a result, your performance improves.

This is not to say that you cannot be proud of your achievement; be a hero when you win or do well, and cherish the moment of recognition or victory. Celebrate your efforts while remaining aware that taunting, bragging, and self-aggrandizement are the patterns of insecure athletes and others who need to promote themselves, yet find it difficult to live up to this inflated image.

To secure honor and glory, give recognition to the greatness of those around you. Notice how others on your team, in your office, or at home, as well as your opponents, will return the gesture. Learning lessons of modesty will help you to become a better person in every aspect of life. There's no need for you to do anything to make others become aware of your greatness. That will happen by itself. When you really think about it, people are usually uncomfortable around those who brag or boast. Have you ever noticed how your unsolicited divulgence of your accomplishments, achievements, or advantages tends to be somewhat offensive, turning others against you? On the other hand, if others seem curious, you shouldn't hesitate to answer their questions and give them information about yourself that could further the conversation. Look for opportunities where you can sincerely affirm yourself and others.

You gain so much more when you relate to others in a modest way rather than being self-centered.

Hold to the inner vision of gradual flowering of potential. Avoid haste. Do not jump ahead blindly. Enjoy the moment of waiting to be!

✳ *Tao Te Ching*

THE CHAMPION knows that deliberate, slow cultivation is the path of success and good fortune. Nothing of value comes quickly, without strong work efforts. Realizing your goals and attaining success are the byproducts of persistence and perspiration. Talent accounts for a mere 5 percent of most achievements. Those who appear to have much talent were once struggling beginners. We all struggle before we become truly great. It is persistence and hard work that lead to achievement and excellence.

Becoming proficient as a team, an individual athlete, or a corporate executive requires a commitment to time, dedication, and excellence, putting in the hours and persisting through any and all setbacks. It usually takes a while before a team in sport or business really gels and begins to play and work consistently well together. You need to be patient and give yourself and the team enough time to become truly great. Persist together for a few years and you'll experience the thrill of victory and success together. Refuse to call a halt to your continual, if slow, progress, and watch as those palm trees finally begin to appear on the horizon. Giving up on the journey is not part of the Way of the Champion, and the best part about persistence is . . . you have complete control over this virtue. You, and no one else, decide whether or not you stay the course. Take charge now!

COMPASSION AND COURAGE

Leaders whose positions endure are those who are the most compassionate; when two armies meet, the one with compassion is the one that tastes victory.
✳ Lao-Tzu

ASSOCIATING WITH CHAMPIONS has taught me the importance of compassion in all aspects of life. In athletics, this translates into one's willingness to play and work with an open heart, being compassionate toward yourself, your coaches, teammates, mates, friends, coworkers, and opponents. Compassion is seeing life through a different lens—in some cases, through others' eyes. It is a form of love and empathy that fuels the fire of the heart and unites teams; as Phil Jackson claims, it is what allowed his world champion Chicago Bulls to sustain high levels of excellence.

According to an ancient Chinese book of wisdom, the *Tao Te Ching,* compassion ignites the courage within, giving one a sense of comfort and security in knowing that when risks are taken, regardless of the outcome, you will survive or thrive. Knowing

that compassion is available, you essentially have permission to fail—not that you would choose such an outcome—as you demonstrate the courage to take an important risk. You gain, with compassion, the safe inner and outer environment that encourages ("instills courage in") you to trust in yourself, your team and coaches, coworkers, family, and friends and to continue to try again and again in the face of adversity.

Then there is courage, which comes from the French word coeur, meaning "heart." Courage allows you to play and perform with heart, to be brave, fearless, tenacious, and relentless. You become more courageous when you know that compassion is available if you fail, make a mistake, or lose.

Adhere to the Zen Buddhist expression "The arrow that hits the bull's-eye is the result of one hundred misses." As an athlete or performer in other arenas of life, it's compassion that helps you to keep shooting the arrows when failure, setbacks, and mistakes are experienced on the journey. Courage becomes compassion's strong emotional and spiritual partner, which helps you realize that you have nothing to lose and everything to gain. Compassion gives you the freedom to take the risk, lose, and learn.

Think about what your world would be like if you treated others and yourself with love and respect. Get "inside the skin" of others and try to understand their suffering without judgment. The word "compassion" literally means to "suffer with." Understand, too, that you are part of something larger than yourself, and setbacks are part of the process of learning to get better. As we know (remember this from "The Success of Failure," in Chapter 7), failure is a good teacher. I notice how my ten greatest successes in sport are the result of a thousand setbacks, mistakes, and failures. Great teams surge ahead of the pack following devastating defeats because they have marinated their nervous systems in a culture of compassion.

This natural, softer approach to sport and other arenas of performance and competition helps you to be more tolerant and accept failure in yourself and others, while continuing to go forward in the exploration of your vast potential. Remember, as I stated previously, there are only two kinds of athletes and performers in the world: those who fail, make mistakes, and commit errors and those who will. Repeat this affirmation often: "Rather than be judgmental and critical of self and others, I choose to put my heart on the line and act with compassion."

BELIEF

*Your inner opponent's greatest advantage is your
lack of belief in your ultimate triumph.*
✳ R. L. WING, *The Art of Strategy*

MOST WHO EXPRESS self-doubt do so because they feel uncertain about outcomes; such uncertainty or lack of belief is warranted because it's impossible for anyone to control the results of any game, event, or situation. No one understands that better than the champion. While one may lack belief in one's power to control results, belief in one's ultimate triumph is essential when triumph is defined as one's willingness to do all that's possible to discover personal greatness. Such belief, according R. L. Wing, is the surest path to victory in the crucial inner game, leading to positive results and outcomes as well.

When you feel a sense of self-doubt and lack of belief, know that you are probably concentrating too much on what you can't control: the outcomes, results, points or goals scored. Refocus, instead, on believing in the following:

❋ Believe in yourself. Know that you have accomplished a great deal. You have skills, strategies, and enough talent to perform well. Simply show up at your event and

BELIEVE that you can demonstrate your current level of fitness. Believe that you are in a position where the best will happen. Expect to have fun and enjoy the process. Believe you will be better because of the experience.

✳ Believe in your teammates or partners. Believe that they, too, are willing to do all they can to make the most of a situation. Have discussions in the group about commitment and desire with regard to going all-out and giving your best. Believe that you are there for each other, especially when the going gets tough.

✳ Believe that your coaches and leaders have the same goals and desires as you and the team, and will work endlessly to give of themselves and do all that's needed in order for everyone to experience their full potential.

✳ Believe that achievement is yours when you believe all of the above. Expect to achieve higher levels of performance. Believe you will have a great experience and terrific season as you put yourself and your teammates and coworkers in position to be the best all of you can be.

Remember this: What you believe you receive. You have within you, now, all that you need to accomplish extraordinary things. Believe this and watch your greatness evolve over time. I want to remind you of the story about the bumblebee in the introduction to this book. The expert aerodynamicist could not calculate how its size, weight, and structure could allow it to fly. But it has, inside, all that it needs to get it done. So do you . . . just believe and begin.

YIELDING

> *Those who are firm and inflexible*
> *are in harmony with dying.*
> *Those who are yielding and receptive*
> *are in harmony with living.*
> *The position of the highly inflexible*
> *will descend;*
> *The position of the yielding and*
> *receptive will ascend.*
>   ✳ *Tao Te Ching*

THE POWER OF YIELDING for a Taoist is best expressed by water. According to the *Tao Te Ching*, nothing in life is more quickly yielding than water, and because of this it is strong and wears away rock.

The Way of the Champion in athletics yields to opposing forces by adapting to change. For example, if an opponent begins to show a full-court press, a blitz, or an attack, you can respond because your preparation has taught you how to be flexible. You need to emulate water and flow in directions that give you the edge. Sun-Tzu tells you to be cre-

ative and flexible, while refusing to give preconceived strategies permission to distract you from yielding, being flexible, and making wise adjustments. Spontaneity is the key to success in these circumstances.

In the martial art aikido, the ability to yield to opposing forces is crucial; the objective is to absorb an attack by blending with its force and using this attacking energy to your advantage. By harmonizing opposing forces, you gain the edge in conflict. This is no different from the objective of an offensive lineman in football who uses the force of the opposition to his advantage by stepping aside and nudging the opponent to the ground. Also, notice how well the philosophy of aikido works when faced with conflict in a personal relationship. Yield by listening to your opponent and understanding (even if not agreeing with) his or her point of view. This strategy often completely disarms the person, and the conflict usually gets resolved more quickly.

Yield to loss, yield to injury, yield to all conflict ... be fluid, pliable, and soft. This will help you to develop a clear mental advantage over those who become psychologically rigid or resistant. Resistance to anything causes tension, anxiety, and stress, which obstruct one's potential. Take a lesson from nature: While rigid tree branches crack during a storm, pliable limbs bend softly and bounce back unharmed. In Chinese lore, bamboo signifies great strength, yet it bends easily in the wind. It flourishes in winter, the harshest of seasons, and happens to be the most versatile of plants, used for food, paper, shelter, and healing in China.

FORTITUDE

THE CHAMPION teaches us that we can't always be strong. We want to show up to perform our best, we want to be fast, want to look good, yet in truth we are not always capable of this. What helps champions during times of frustration, strife, uncertainty, and disappointment is the virtue of fortitude, a sense of quiet strength and confidence, a deep trust and faith, and a simple, lasting willingness or stubbornness to endure.

For athletes, fortitude is often the ingredient that gets them through a slump, a poorly played half, the unexpected, a losing streak, a disappointing result, a series of injuries, or an elimination from a playoff.

Then there is a crisis with friends or family, a rejection of your book by a publisher, and any other trying circumstance. Fortitude is the answer. This strong spiritual weapon has saved large groups of people throughout the world who still exist culturally because they have stubbornly refused to give in.

Again, think about how bamboo bends in the wind and survives, while the huge, strong oak breaks. Fortitude is your ability to bend in the wind, to endure life's hardships and battles on and off the court, to get back on your feet each time you are down.

To exhibit fortitude, think of being brave. Athletics, as do other situations in life, throw challenges your way, which are standing invitations to be brave. For example, to win his fifth straight Tour de France, Lance Armstrong overcame pileups, dehydration, saddle sores, broken equipment—not to mention the Pyrenees and 197 other riders—demonstrating his virtue of fortitude. His fortitude is no different from that of the seventy-year-old grandmother who ran into a flame-engulfed apartment to rescue her cat.

Being brave is the spiritual space of displaying courage, taking risks during an event, and being strong in the face of pain. To help with this, look around you during a game, and you'll see a teammate being brave. Imitate that athlete for a while. Then look around and notice how others are following you. Bravery is an integral part of fortitude. Fortitude has won world wars—it can help you to endure and to be successful in your sport, career, and life.

SACRIFICE

CHAMPIONS SACRIFICE and demand more from themselves, while other athletes live in a comfort zone, avoiding doing anything that is uncomfortable—particularly avoiding doing all that it takes to raise the bar and achieve higher levels in sport. They refuse to sacrifice or suffer. They live a risk-free life. In the comfort zone, they stagnate.

Remember this truth: If you do each day what you always do, you will never expand. If you sacrifice and demand that you do more, you will continue to improve. Your performance in practice, games, competition, and business is either below the bar of excellence or above it. Being above it demands sacrifice and suffering. You need to choose where you wish to be. If you want positive change—to improve your "game"— you're the only one who can make that happen, by your willingness to make the appropriate sacrifice.

The following affirmation will help you to stay aligned with this virtue: "I refuse to simply go through the motions. I am willing to sacrifice and demand more of myself, out of *respect* and *pride*, and I commit to following through on these self-demands."

RESPECT

R ESPECT FOR THE GAME, respect for self, team-mates, coaches, and opponents is a virtue practiced by all champions, whether they are among the best or basically unknown. Being disrespectful is inexcusable on or off the court.

Quin Snyder, head men's basketball coach at the University of Missouri, recognizes the importance of respect as a virtue for champion athletes. He has one rule for his team and has consistently enforced it: SHOW RESPECT. If one of his athletes comes late for practice, doesn't know the plays, fails to hustle, misses class, receives poor grades, dresses improperly, or behaves inappropriately, he is not being respectful.

In Quin's first season as head coach, one of his star players mouthed off during practice, almost as if to test his new coach. The player's frustration was apparent, but his approach was unacceptable. Rather than react from his ego and chastise the athlete in front of his teammates, Quin went silent, looked at the player for ten seconds (which seemed like an eternity to everyone on the court), and then resumed play. After practice, Quin and this player met face-to-face. Coach Snyder talked to this young man, telling him, "I understand your frustration, but I will not tolerate such outbursts." With tears of regret, the athlete apologized. Through respect for the athlete and the team, Quin demonstrated to the player and everyone on the court his strength, control, and focus that day. The team's respect for their rookie coach grew immensely.

The point to be made is that mutual respect is essential for high-level performance. Winning is difficult, inconsistent, and volatile in the absence of respect. Champions, even if they don't win, know that without respect, they never will.

Respect, in its most global sense, is really about your relationships with all aspects and in all realms of sport and life. A healthy relationship with yourself is demonstrated by respect through integrity and the use of positive self-talk, while visualizing being the best you can be and doing all that it takes. Regarding your relationships with teammates, office workers, and family, you show respect through communication, forgiveness, and bringing out their best. Your relationship with the coach, manager, or boss, if built on trust and loyalty, becomes one of mutual respect. Then there is the respect for opponents, built on a relationship of compassion and partnership, as you seek together your individual and collective greatness. Sun-Tzu asks that you take this respect to a deeper level by giving your opponent the opportunity to lose with dignity. For example, "call off the hounds" by matching the opponent with similar athletes once the game is under control. And, never press when the

opposition is desperate. Finally, there is your relationship to the game, built on respect for what it teaches,
as well as the opportunity to grow and expand in this
microcosmic classroom for all of life.

True respect is earned when you demonstrate the
solid, virtuous qualities of the champion. It requires
you to respect others as you would like to be respected.

LESSONS AS AFFIRMATIONS

✳ I am aware of the power of modesty to bring success
   over time.
✳ I do not hesitate to give recognition to those around me.
✳ My ability to persist when all seems bleak enables me
   to act like a champion.
✳ My journey as a champion is filled with compassion
   for myself, my team, and my opponent.
✳ I have the courage to take good risks in order to
   improve.
✳ My setbacks and failures are my teachers.
✳ Because I can yield like bamboo, I have the mental
   edge over all who are rigid.
✳ Fortitude is my ability to demonstrate quiet strength.
✳ I trust that, regardless of circumstances, I will endure.
✳ When I demand more from myself, I show I am seri-
   ous about raising my level of play.
✳ As a champion, I demonstrate respect to myself and
   others.

QUESTIONS ON THE QUEST:

✳ When do you tend to exhibit a lack of compassion for
   yourself and others? What specifically can you do to
   change that?

* What five things can you demand of yourself this week that will stimulate the very best in your performance?
* What do you do each day that demonstrates respect for yourself, teammates, coworkers, and family?

9. Lessons on Opposites

All existence is circular, a Yin-Yang process where black
and white become richly gray.
✴ Deng Ming-Dao, *Tao Wisdom*

CHAMPIONS, characteristically, are quite good at thinking outside the box. Yet most of society teaches that when a choice between two opposing forces exists, there is a strong gravitational pull toward one or the other. Western minds are conditioned to be dualistic; we are most comfortable amid contrasts and distinctions. For example, you are either a champion or a novice, beautiful or ugly, simple or complex, sharp or dull. The Tao, however, makes no distinction. Something is not yin or yang . . . it is both simultaneously. Bamboo, once again, is powerful and delicate, soft yet hard. The mentor-teacher is a student, yet the student teaches the teacher how to do the job well.

In athletics, grasping this subtle paradox can strengthen your competitive edge. A champion is a beginner, open to discovering just how great he or she can be. A champion is both a winner and a loser, as you clearly read in "The Success of Failure," in Chapter 7. Understanding these paradoxical mysteries helps you to develop greater strength and higher levels of participation in athletics.

For example, if you are too yang, that is, too focused on outcome and results, you can become nervous, tense, anxious, and stressed. This leads to mistakes, setbacks, and possible illness and injury, because you refuse to listen to what nature is saying. If you are too yin, that is passive or self-conscious, you can become timid and nonassertive. This can result in being hesitant and unfulfilled, failing to reach the vast boundaries of your potential.

When you integrate these seemingly conflicting forces, you experience a balancing of the yin and yang currents that will keep you aligned and in harmony with the true natural way of sports. By so doing, you learn to develop the right timing and become more willing to let the "game" come to you, let it evolve at its own pace and tempo. In this consciousness, there is a place for both aggression and passivity, speed and slowing down. The champion athlete understands this need to neutralize the duality, and uses it to gain the advantage in all competitive arenas.

You are about to see how slowing down can help you to arrive sooner, how soft is strong, how less is more, how the body thinks and the mind dances, how effort can be effortless, and how you can have limits yet go beyond. As you recall, when you lose, you actually win. Here we go.

SLOWER IS FASTER

CAN YOU IMAGINE viewing beautiful flowers while racing downhill on your mountain bike? Most of life's situations demand that you try to match your speed to the task at hand. Our lives have become so used to a fast pace that the thought of slowing down is frightening. My twenty-year-old son wants me to spend an excessive amount of money on a new computer system that will save me thirty-five seconds each time I go online. It's not good enough that my six-year-old dinosaur retrieves the same amount of data in one minute that would have taken my father one week to gather.

Being a champion means having the patience to allow change, growth, and improvement to take place when they are supposed to, not when we think they should. The Tao encourages a calm observation of the natural unfolding of events. Most of your potential usually blossoms in a gradual way. Patience, according to Lao-Tzu, is the ability to accept the slow flow of the journey.

John Wooden, wise and thoughtful coach of champions, advises us to avoid looking for quick improvement. When you improve a little each day, big things eventually occur. That's the only way it happens, and because of this, it lasts.

When I was training as a distance runner in Boulder, Colorado, I wanted to accelerate my growth as a national-class athlete. To do so, I worked out three times a day, seven days a week. After four consecutive months of this lunacy, my body finally gave out, and I became both physically and mentally fried. I withdrew from my sport for six months and proceeded to sink into the abyss. Once I recovered, it took a full year to match my former level of mental, emotional, spiritual, and physical fitness. That eighteen months taught me that I needed to enter into a new time zone: slow down in order to speed up. I learned how to listen to the messages of my body and mind about fatigue, soreness, tightness, pain, lack of motivation or enthusiasm, and loss of confidence and focus. Today, I must remind myself that through the inner qualities of consistent, deliberate, steady, slow movement, the tortoise arrives sooner than the quicker yet more sporadic, inconsistent hare.

Sun-Tzu, in *The Art of War*, advises that you notice the natural flow of events and then act accordingly. This requires constant vigilance as you monitor your progress with regard to levels of energy, fatigue, soreness, staleness, slumps, plateaus, spurts, enthusiasm, and burnout. Too much, too soon, that familiar "hurry up" sickness, invariably leads to injury, illness, burnout, or depression—nature's way of telling you to slow down, reevaluate, and take a break. This is the Way of the Champion.

NOT DOING IS DOING

Success is often gained by not doing battle, the strategy is as much in knowing what not to do as it is in knowing what to do.

✳ Sun-Tzu

HERE IS THE ART of not doing, where the Tao wisdom helps us to understand that "less is more." The Way of the Champion encourages you to engage in battle when others are vulnerable, and to not attack when you are. From this, the champion realizes the vulnerability of overdoing and when to be moderate.

The temptation to overdo in sports and life is very enticing and attractive. However, all that you gain from being excessive is drastically offset by the accumulation of tightness, tension, stress, unbalance, and fatigue, creating a debt that needs to be paid back by taking time off to rest, or you will eventually pay the price of failure, setbacks, and burnout.

Mike, a conscientious runner, has been at it for twenty years with the single-minded goal (which is now his obsession) of breaking three hours in the marathon. He has run every day at a good clip, with weekly long jaunts of eighteen or more miles. He has run a best of 3:08, a frustratingly "close but no cigar" performance. Recently, I suggested he consider a more moderate program of fifty to sixty miles a week, rather than his usual seventy-five miles, with a long run every fourteen days. He now takes one day a week off and pushes the pace on only two runs in a seven-day period. He is now convinced that not doing so much is, indeed, actually doing more, because he recently ran a personal best of 2:57 on a difficult course.

Many who train their bodies diligently are beginning to realize that not only are there spiritual and psychological advantages to not doing so much, but some important physiological benefits as well. For example, try to run, swim, bike, or walk every other day, rather than seven days a week, and give your body and mind a chance to recuperate. You can begin to use the "stress then rest" maxim for conditioning, alternating workout days with total days off in between. If you are constantly fatigued and your overall performance is down, try reducing your workout time each day and notice the improvement.

An accomplished jazz musician once told me that truly good music is the result of the *space between notes*. The pause makes it what it is. Musical pauses are not a lack of action; they are an integral part of the action. So it is with your training and work schedule. Getting in good shape, being at your best regardless of your sport or career, is the result of the *rest* (pause) or space between the intervals of work. Your cellular structure is fragile and requires periods of rest. Like a champion, you need to learn how to "fondle" your body into shape, as opposed to excessively forcing or pushing it there.

One may argue that to be world-class in any walk of life, there is no room for moderation. Many believe that you excel with excess. Hordes of athletes devote every waking hour to training. Corporate executives are known for devoting sixty to seventy hours per week to furthering their career. They may win gold or get the contract promotion, but they also run the risk of losing on other fronts. For example, young tennis stars, dynamic skaters, and gymnasts often become unbalanced in their approach. They skip school, opting for correspondence courses so they can eat, drink, and sleep their obsession. Theirs becomes an artificial existence, an emotional wasteland of excess, far away from the crucial natural maturation process of adolescence. Few of these young athletes go on to succeed; many more wind up wasting their lives. Even for those who do well, success takes its toll in so many other ways.

In a recent Olympiad, a U.S. gold medalist in swimming was asked, "Where do you go from here?" "Far away from pools" was the instant response. He proceeded to relate how much he had sacrificed on his road to fame and intimated that it might not have been worth it. He complained about the lack of moderation and balance in his life. He craved "not doing" any workouts.

In sport, as in other arenas of life, your mind will tell your body to do more than it can handle, but your body and health will have the final say. The *Tao Te Ching's* wisdom helps to override this tendency through moderation. The Chinese calligraphic symbols for moderation point to the middle, thus preventing excess while neutralizing opposites: "Less is more."

LITTLE IS LARGE

THERE IS A BEAUTIFUL SAYING that helps me to focus on what is important in my athletic and personal life: "From little streams come large rivers." This Zenlike phrase echoes the sentiments of coach John Wooden: "Over the years I have become convinced that attention to little details makes the difference between champions and near champions." He talks about concentrating on all those little things that make you play well, as opposed to focusing on the score or stats. And when you do, whether in sports or life, good things happen. For example, an athlete told me he was so fixated on demonstrating the little things, that he didn't realize his basketball team was about to blow out the opponent by twenty-five points.

The following is an excerpt from an e-mail communication between a collegiate basketball athlete and myself over her concerns with results, points, and outcomes, to the exclusion of the little things:

Vicki, on game day, meditate in the morning if possible. Continue to visualize and feel yourself doing the little things. Play, over and over in your head, your 'highlight mind movie' . . . i.e., clips of when you play your best. Go into the game NOT to score (sounds to me like you still do that) but to demonstrate all the little skills and tactics you KNOW you can control. Concentrate ONLY on doing good things . . . shoot when it's there but stop trying to get points, assists, etc. Stay connected to being brave, courageous, and deliberate, as well as to why you love the GAME and forget about your coach, Dad, me, or teammates . . . OK?"

Her response: "Hey, Jerry, how are you doing? This past week I had some great practices and we played on Saturday and I had a great game, I felt like my old self again, and more importantly, I was having fun. Even my friends and family who were at the game said it looked like I was having fun out there again. Thanks for the advice. It really is all about the little things, isn't it?"

Yes, Vicki, not only for you, but for all of us other performers on any of life's stages as well. In fact, I observe that the strong consistent performance of the little things outdoes brilliant tactics performed occasionally and marginally. Coaches continue to inform me that the greatest obstacle to the team's success is their consistent refusal to do the little things. To help you address this notion of little streams to big rivers, answer this question: What are the five to ten little things about your game, work, or home that, if attended to and performed consistently, would make you feel happy and successful at what you do? Write these little things on an index card and read it as an affirmation each day: "When I (fill in the blank with these items), I create many opportunities to experience success, regardless of the outcome."

OPPONENTS ARE PARTNERS

IN THE BEGINNING of the book, I emphasized the importance of knowing your opponents in order to gain the advantage for potential victory against them. There is another, deeper, more evolved notion that relates to knowing your opponents as partners in a relationship of cooperation. It becomes a partnership of offering each other the best you've got, to help bring out the best in each other.

Consider that the word "competition" comes from a Latin root meaning "to seek together." When I view my relationship with opponents as a partnership, I offer my absolutely strongest attack, giving them the opportunity to respond and bring their best to the table. Anything short of my fiercest blow is a sign of my disrespect, and I cease to be, in Zen terminology, a "worthy opponent."

I remember competing in a national 15K cross-country championship race in Houston, Texas. Many of the runners were talking about the ways they could defeat their closest rivals. They alluded to the killer instinct and how important it was to compete well. When I approached the pre-race favorite, I proceeded to shock him by saying, "I hope you have a great race." Confused by the words, the favorite inquired as to why I felt that way. I told him, "The better you run, the better I will, too." The favorite did win the race, and I claimed third, running my fastest time for the distance—and, in the process, pushing the winner to one of his greatest victories.

I was simply being a "worthy opponent," helping the opposition to do well and running my best because of him. Because of this, our relationship grew stronger in many ways. Through his subsequent encouragement and kind words, I reached levels I never thought were possible. We both got to know each other, our strengths and weaknesses, and used this information to race at higher levels together. I loved this opponent; why do so many of us waste emotional and physical energy hating those we compete against? Why focus on their demise? It may seem to help, but in the long run, the champion knows this approach is counterproductive, because anger, hate, and force diminish your concentration, dilute your energy, and lead to your downfall.

Remember, change your mind-set now: View all athletic and business competitors as partners who, because of their outstanding work and performance, help you to understand yourself more fully and challenge you to step up and demonstrate your best. Begin to experience the powerful connection and relationship with your opponent in the world of competitive athletics and life. For example, on your next training bike ride, see your group as a partnership. The better they ride, the better you will ultimately be. Feel the advantages in athletics and business of working together, with synergistic competition providing a surplus of energy for positive performance. Know your opposition in this new, refreshing way, not only as a competitor, but as a partner as well.

SOFT IS STRONG

YOU WOULD THINK that a soft muscle is not strong, yet as with other paradoxes, the opposite is true. Try doing three push-ups and make your arms tight and hard as you proceed. Take a minute break, make your muscles soft yet firm, and repeat the process. The second set was probably easier.

The next time you pump iron, don't try hard. Relax your muscles, take a deep breath, and gradually lift the weights in a soft yet firm manner. Notice the difference?

Running up hills is no different. My twelve-year-old was running his first cross-country race. I was standing at the bottom of the racecourse's only hill, and as he went by me in fifth place, I shouted, "Bren, relax your shoulders and soften your eyes." (We had talked about this strategy during his warmup.) He passed all runners on that hill and maintained his lead for a victory in his inaugural race.

Champions realize that a "softer" 90 percent effort sometimes produces better, faster, stronger results than trying to give it your all. Years ago, champion track coach Bud Winter from San José State University would get his Stallions runners to go faster by having them relax and make their bodies soft. By running at 90 percent effort, Olympians John Carlos and Tommy Smith became the anchors for what became known as "Speed City." You need to relax in order to max, so to speak. Gritting your teeth and squeezing your hands creates tense muscles and inhibits performance. *The Art of War* reminds you that the calm, reserved, relaxed performer is the one who wins, all things being somewhat equal.

Here is a thought: As you age, teeth, which are hard, become brittle and break; tongues, which are soft, last. Throw hard pasta against the wall and watch it shatter. Cook it, make it soft, and notice how it clings when thrown against that same wall.

Look for ways to "soften" your approach and be stronger in any arena of life.

EFFORT IS EFFORTLESS

> *Follow the path of least resistance if you want to be victorious.*
>
> ✳ Sun-Tzu

A S WITH the above paradoxes and opposites, here is a concept diametrically opposed to everything you have learned about competitive athletics and achievement in all of life: The way to achieve triumph more effectively is through tactical strategies that eliminate or minimize conflict and resistance. This ancient wisdom is the essence of *The Art of War.* It is considered the art of effortless effort.

For example, when you make an effort to descend a rocky trail on a mountain bike, you try to pick the best "line"—the one that offers the least resistance, the least amount of effort. It is not always the shortest distance between two points, but it is the one that gets you to the bottom safely, quickly, and with the least amount of trouble, resistance, or conflict. It is an approach that requires you to apply much less effort and to yield to the forces in nature, rather than become rigid and self-destruct on the trail. In Chinese, this effortless effort paradox is called *wu-wei*, meaning "do not do that which is not natural." It is not natural to push, force, or fight the flow. Blend effortlessly with all force as your effort becomes effortless.

In sport, the champion adopts this principle and knows that rigidity sets in when you give an all-out effort. When you want to go faster or climb stronger, don't force it to happen. Relax and focus your effort on the execution of fluid, technically correct movement. Less effort creates more output. For example, let's say that you are trying to ride a steep hill. Rather than apply forceful effort, imagine that you glide up rather than push yourself up, using imaginary helium balloons on your shoulders that gently help you to float to the top.

When you feel yourself trying to do well in an event, focus on the joy and excitement of what you're doing, on the process of how you can perform well in the moment. Push less for results, and notice how things go more smoothly. Tell yourself that you're working or competing to enjoy the execution of a well-thought-out plan; don't perseverate on the outcome. You practically have to "not care" yet not be totally careless in the delicate balance of effortless effort. Martial artists have understood for centuries that the less effort you exert, the more proficient you will become in all that you do.

Let me remind you that a fish wisely swims downstream, taking the most effortless way. Seek the path of least resistance and you gain the edge.

INSIDE IS OUTSIDE

WHEN YOU THINK ABOUT IT, all that happens to you externally seems to be a mere reflection of what's at work internally. Therefore, we have the paradox: What's going on inside is really what is happening outside. According to the Tao, all that begins within creates the "ripple effect," stretching outward, touching all things in its wake. How does this concept impact you in a practical way?

As a champion in athletics or life, the more you feel inwardly successful, having a handle on self-doubt and possessing a strong sense of self, the less need you have to succeed externally. The less need you feel to succeed externally, the less you will experience stress, tension, and anxiety. The less stress, tension, and anxiety you have about having to win or achieve, the more relaxed and focused you become and, under these conditions, the more successful you become externally. What I notice about all champions is that when inner peace and high self-esteem are part of their journey, they consistently perform at the peak of their abilities. Good stuff within creates similar good stuff externally, and vice versa. Inside is truly outside. All greatness, wellness, and success start within.

BODY THINKING, MIND DANCING

O R IS IT THE OPPOSITE? The body dances and the mind thinks. Here is yet another paradox that makes you stop short in your tracks and say . . . this can't be. But can it?

In this closing of the chapter, I briefly want to tell you about my best-selling book, with Chungliang Al Huang, *Thinking Body, Dancing Mind*, in which I never once talked about the meaning of this provocative title. It is a nice way to demonstrate the lesson on opposites.

First of all, as an athlete, your training in sport has allowed your body to develop muscle memory or innate intelligence as a result of the consistent repetition of familiar motions, actions, and skills. This is the "thinking body," the body that responds instinctively to a variety of physical circumstances. Shooting a basketball involves numerous specific mechanical muscle responses. The body "knows" how to execute a shot without the mind thinking about how it is done. The mind, on the other hand, dances with this body's knowledge when it refrains from judgment or criticism and the result is one of harmonious interaction. Sometimes, the mind will think "Oh, no, I'm hurting," or "I stink," or "I can't," or "I'm not deserving of . . ." In this way, the critical, negative mind sabotages everything that the body tries to do from its knowledge base, and rather than dance, it begins to think too much.

The champion, without question, practices the

thinking body, dancing mind approach. The champion who does this successfully has the competitive advantage. You can practice this approach by using positive self-talk and visualizing yourself playing your sport as you know how . . . trusting your body. Such talk and images will keep you on track.

LESSONS AS AFFIRMATIONS

* I demonstrate consistent, deliberate, steady movement yet arrive just in time.
* I listen to the messages of my body and mind, and make adjustments accordingly.
* I look for times when less is more. Moderation is the key.
* My opponent is my partner as we seek together our individual greatness.
* Aware that soft is strong, I can't go wrong.
* I make less effort and gain more. I follow the path of least resistance.
* Do not do that which is not natural. Go with the flow.
* I let my mind dance with my thinking body.

QUESTIONS ON THE QUEST:

* Under what circumstances in athletics, business, or life would less be more for you?
* When, for you, in sports, business, and personal relationships, is soft actually strong?
* In what specific ways do you sabotage your body's wisdom?
* What specific things do you need to do in your game, work environment, or home life in order to go with the flow?
* What three actions can you take to demonstrate healthy moderation as a champion?

IV

THE WAY OF TEAM UNITY AND LEADERSHIP

*Under the right conditions . . . justice, order, leadership
and morale . . . a small team could prevail over a large
group. Those who establish a viable group will win even
if they are small. The key to all operations is harmony
with people.*

✳ Sun-Tzu

STRATEGIST SUN-TZU believed that the key to
triumph in battle is unity of purpose and heart.
This statement has tremendous relevance for
coaches, athletes, teams, businesses, and families.
Tao wisdom teaches that connection, team spirit,
and cohesion are vital aspects for victory both on
the field and in all of life. In an age when most of us
seem self-absorbed, when "me not we" is a mantra,
we can use such wisdom and practice the virtue of
selflessness in many ways. Think of the familylike
the cohesion demonstrated by the 1980 U.S.
Olympic hockey team or the 1999 women's World
Cup champion soccer team, whose hearts and
souls were forged together on their journey to victory. Both teams were united by their willingness to
embrace unity, oneness, and the team spirit, placing these warriors in position to realize their
dreams. Creating team unity and cohesion takes
work. Even if your "team" doesn't seem to possess
natural team chemistry, this quality can be learned
and instilled. The following strategies in Part IV
will help you to develop conscious leadership and
team cohesion for greater success.

10. Lessons on Team Harmony

The Tao of operations lies in harmonizing people. When people are in harmony, they will fight naturally, without being coerced to do so.
✳ Zhuge Liang, Chinese strategist

THE EMPHASIS on the power of a harmonious group is an important feature that has made *The Art of War* one of the most widely read books among generals, corporate CEOs, and athletic coaches throughout the world. The Chinese book of change, the *I Ching*, teaches that the human spirit is nourished by a sense of connectedness and unity.

The champion is well aware of how synergy and cooperative action impact the success of teams. It is the key to team effectiveness in any arena of life. In his insightful book *Playing for Keeps*, David Halberstam talks about how, at the University of North Carolina, under the guidance of coach Dean Smith, "everything was built around the concept of team. . . . In the long run he believed that you went further by working as a team and sacrificing individuality to team effort . . . it would serve his players better later in their lives." Who could argue with such a successful program . . . and the success of its graduates twenty years later?

Furthering these thoughts, coach Phil Jackson believes that good teams become great ones when the members trust each other enough to get beyond the "me" for the "we." The key to such a shift, in Jackson's mind, is the Zen notion of selflessness; more about this concept later.

Students of history can point out how world cultures strive for spiritual togetherness, to harmonize the hearts and minds of the people. The *Tao Te Ching* reminds us that cultures that eternally exist do so because they exist for each other. Sports teams, business organizations, and families that exist for each other tend to be around for a long time. The following lessons on harmony have been used successfully by thousands of successful, long-lasting champions.

TEAM MAGIC

WHEN I WORK with teams that demonstrate many of the qualities of a champion, I notice something special about them. They exude a certain magic . . . how they walk, talk, run, play. It's different in a special way. The following passage describes my experience after being with such a team during an action-packed, intense final-four weekend. I gave each member a copy, and I want you to have a sense about their dance, their way, one that mesmerized all who came to watch. I wish we all could experience the magic of such a team:

In my view, the athletes who play on this team do so because there is a magic to it, one that is hard to find in life. Partly, this magic resides in the physical sensation and pleasure, of catching a ball on the run, sprinting to the goal for a score. Part of the magic is in the psychological realm where we feel the trust, security, and confidence from being together all season. And in the spiritual domain, it is the safe, comfortable place created to help us take risks and look foolish or fail, so necessary to discover what we are made of, the juice of life, a way of being, not only on the field, court, arena, but in the larger game of life. There is not only the relationship with team, coach, self but our relationship to the stick, the bat, the ball . . . all an extension of our hearts, our souls, an expression of who we are. There is also an aesthetic component of the team, one that demonstrates the absolutely most beautiful way of playing and competing. Just as ballet is the most beautiful way of moving the body between two points, your team is to your sport as ballet is to walking. So many other teams wish they could dance like you rather than experience a dance form more rigid, forceful, less fluid, and contrived. These are forms without soul, without heart, without courage. When they *see you, they discover a more disciplined, beautiful, flowing way, free of fear, filled with compassion, all of which fills the void, the holes in the soul. They crave your dance and are not sure what it is or how you're being. They just know they are tired of being the wallflowers in the big dance. They want a piece of the magic you own, yet, until they let go of the need to fight you, beat you, destroy you and simply play the game or dance the dance, the magic will be forever elusive.*

They did win the national championship, but more importantly, they won the hearts of all who came to experience their demonstration of passion and love for the game. They were being champions even before the outcome was decided. The next year, at another final four, the team t-shirts read: DANCE ON. They did and won, once again.

GEESE IN FLIGHT

Champion-like teams are very much like a flock of geese migrating to warmer climates. First of all, the geese fly together, in a V formation, in order to help each other conserve energy. Because of this, they use less effort, and as a result can then fly 71 percent farther. This is the same principle used by top-notch cycling teams who share the work as they aerodynamically cruise through the course.

Geese in flight are continually "honking" as they go. To an observer, this is nothing more than an annoyance. For the birds, these are the sweet sounds of encouragement and positive chatter; they could be saying "way to go, big bird, keep it up, looking strong, you can do it." Champion teams mimic their fine feathered friends in this way.

And the most impressive behavior of all reflects their deep caring and compassion the geese have for each other. When a "teammate" gets injured or sick during the journey, a small group stays behind to nurture their buddy back to health. They are "there" for each other to help during a crisis. So it is with champion teams; when the going gets tough, the tough get going and contribute in a big way to relieve each other's pain, to help those in need.

When champions model these behaviors, they also fly high like the geese. The V formation then becomes the universal sign for victory, which champions experience in the process, in the here and now. Again, the wisdom of *The Art of War* tells you that a cohesive, harmonic team with high morale often will defeat a more talented group that lacks such qualities. The truth is, it is difficult to beat a team that plays like a team. And, there's nothing more beautiful than watching and experiencing a group of inspired, unified, cohesive, athletes playing together for a common cause, one heart, one soul.

158 STARTING AND STOPPING

HERE IS A GROUP EXERCISE for creating team harmony that I learned from a good friend and colleague, Dr. Alan Goldberg. I use it often to get a group to be on the same page and work together more closely. It's called "Stop, Start, and Continue."

The exercise is done in any private, intimate meeting room. It consists of a series of three questions:

1. What are we doing now that we have to stop doing, as a team, group, family, to build team unity and to function at a higher level?

2. What are we not doing now that we have to start doing, as a team, group, family, to build team unity and to function at a higher level?

3. What are we doing that we need to continue doing, as a team, group, family, to keep our cohesion and unity strong?

The results of this exercise are powerful. You may want to record the responses on a master sheet, give a copy to everyone, and ask them to read it each day for the following week. Check in with everyone within the week to see how they are managing their tasks. This exercise exposes what's going well and what needs work, and provides some creative ways to address these issues. Accountability and responsibility are central to the mission of this work.

There is a poignant Chinese fable that demonstrates the power of working together: The story has it that heaven and hell are exactly alike. Both are enormous banquets with every wonderful dish imaginable covering numerous round tables. The diners are given five-foot-long chopsticks. In hell, the diners give up trying to manipulate these giant utensils and starve. In heaven, everyone simply feeds the person across the table. How does this story relate to teamwork in athletics or life?

SHARED REFLECTION

> *Attain the highest openness;*
> *Maintain the deepest harmony.*
> ✳ *Tao Te Ching*

THE TAO TEACHES YOU to notice the patterns in your life, to reflect upon what is happening with you and others in your life, and to be open and honest with your feelings. Reflection enables you to take time out and "check in" with yourself and others as athletes and friends. You need to be able to appreciate how far each of you has come, and why. The Way of the Champion understands

that such periodic shared reflection with teammates, coworkers, and family members promotes team harmony, trust, and cohesion. I have used the following exercises for many years with teams in athletics and business to accomplish this goal. It works well with families, too.

THE CIRCLE OF APPRECIATION

There is no question that the participants absolutely love this experience. I use it sparingly, choosing significant times during a season, such as an important tournament, the last game of the season, or when there seems to be low morale. This will help the participants to feel closer and good about themselves, by generating powerful performance-enhancing emotions. I have used it with people from the ages of thirteen and up. You need to allow at least an hour to complete the exercise. Do not use this if there are many unresolved conflicts within the group. I divide everyone into a circle of fifteen to thirty participants. If there are more than this, you could have two or more groups in numerous circles. Feel free to mix male and female if they train together. I begin by telling the group that this exercise has been used by several great championship teams at the professional and collegiate ranks, and that it will help them to compete at a higher level. We start with anyone in the circle, who turns to the person to the left and makes a few positive comments about anything he or she

admires, likes, and respects about that person. Those in the circle need to understand that trivial remarks such as "I like how you dress" are inappropriate. Try something like "I love your work ethic. You really motivate us. I respect your way of giving to everyone," or "I feel like you are a brother (sister) to me. I know I can count on you." Comments need to be sincere, personal, and positive. It's not essential that you like the person; simply find something nice, relevant, and true to express. After everyone has had a chance to contribute (coaches as well), reverse the direction, if time allows. To further guide the group, I mention that they should keep their comments to no more than a minute or two. I am not rigid about this, however. My experience has been that, once they get into this, they don't want to stop; you can't keep them quiet; they crave such feedback and deserve it. You should not do this if strapped for time. I tell coaches that we need to not feel pressure to leave. It's a rare opportunity for most, and it feels terrific, so let it flow.

GREATEST MEMORY CIRCLE

Again, we begin this exercise in a circle. It's similar to the above experience, yet usually not as deeply personal. Have each athlete focus on something significant that occurred during the season, a time of joy, elation, sadness, disappointment, winning, or losing. As they recall and speak about these moments to each other, everyone in the group will begin to feel a special connection and bond. Memories can be individual or team-related. Again, encourage the athletes to avoid trivial comments. As with the Circle of Appreciation, start and go around the circle to your left (the heart is on the left side of the body). Coaches are included in the discussion. Needless to say, this is best done toward the conclusion of a season.

POWER OF THE CIRCLE

THE SYMBOLIC USE of the circle in sport and for life is significant. Obviously, we talk about a "round" of golf, played with a tiny round ball that goes in a circular cup. "Round ball" is about basketball, also referred to as "Hoops." You shoot three pointers from behind the arc. There is the circle at center court where the game begins. Motion offense requires the interchange of players moving in circular patterns. In baseball, a home run is called a "round tripper." The mound is circular, and the pitcher winds up in a circular fashion, delivering a round ball to a batter who hits it and circles the bases. Everywhere you look, the circle is present.

Its significance with respect to team unity is enormous. My work with groups always begins with a large circle, or several smaller versions. Of all the symbols, it is the circle that is most associated with Zen, Tao, and Native American tradition. I tell my groups that the circle is a sacred bond that brings us together in one unified fashion. There is no beginning and no end, yet it is complete. Nothing else has this special quality.

I talk about the relevance of the circle for our journey. As we go around the circumference in the group circle, I point out that we wind up where we began. The circular journey is one where you spiral upward while constantly revisiting certain familiar themes with greater wisdom, vision, and perspective, more developed because of the experience. We are changed athletes and people from whom we once were.

The circle gives us the chance to appreciate the center of "emptiness" within its circumference. The "beginner's mind," like the inner circle, is empty and full of infinite potential, like our team. I emphasize the importance of being empty, open, and receptive to new ideas just as the middle of the circle is open and ready for the entrance of good things happening.

And finally, what better way to communicate and connect with each other than in a circle, where you can look in each other's eyes, the windows to the soul, and be accountable to the team? We connect physically in the circle, as well, reaching out, holding hands or locking arms, and forming an uninterrupted solid circle, all together in the spirit of oneness. "Let the circle be unbroken," as the song so wisely states.

THE CHAMPION TEAM

MANY TEAMS want to be champions. I am quick to remind them that being a champion is not about becoming. It's a spiritual practice of connecting to the actions, behaviors, and virtues of the champion's way. I say to them: You are a championship-level team if:

* You know who you are ... you *self-define* and act on it every day.

* You share the same dream, vision, passion, and willingness to do *all that it takes* (including diminished roles, etc.) in order to be successful.

* You challenge each other (all-out efforts) in practice, knowing that making it difficult for each other helps everyone to improve. Be fierce, bold, and courageous in workouts and you'll be that way in an event.

* You all accept a leadership role in your own way, rather than rely on only a few to do the work. Bring hope, enthusiasm, and fire each day. Leadership is a daily practice.

* You walk *side by side* over many miles of rough terrain, win or lose, happy or sad . . . it all serves to bring you closer. Share your appreciation of each other out loud (Circle of Appreciation).

* You support each other to take the necessary risks to become great, even if you look foolish, feel uncomfortable. Compassion is the one virtue that enables a team to sustain success over time.

* You are not afraid to ask for help. Teams are strongest when they understand the interdependent nature of things. Shouting "help" on defense is acceptable; so should it be in all other aspects of the game, and of life.

* You pursue victory in a context of cooperation, friendship, support, mutual respect, and compassion. This is "truth," learned through team sports.

Know that each of these items is filled with concepts and thoughts that can be brought to the table for discussion at team or group meetings. For example, spend an hour on item number one by asking: "Who are we as a team?" When the adjectives pour out, ask them what actions or behaviors they can perform that will help to demonstrate these words, to make the words come alive on the field during a game. Go through each item and let the group give its input with regard to its relevancy to the team.

LESSONS AS AFFIRMATIONS

✷ Magic happens to my team or group when we stay connected to our love and passion for the game and demonstrate them each day.
✷ Working together, each one becomes so much more.
✷ Compassion is the glue that binds my team or group.
✷ I look for ways to work with my teammates and coworkers and raise our level of play.
✷ It is crucial to take the time to check in with my team or group and express appreciation for who they are.
✷ I honor the significance of the circle as a sacred bond that ties us all together.
✷ The circle reminds me of the journey and the infinite potential available when minds are open.

QUESTIONS ON THE QUEST:

✷ What two things can I do today to help make my team or group special?
✷ In what ways is my team or group magic?

* What is the greatest memory I have about my team or group?
* What are three things I appreciate about my team or group?
* Why can we achieve our goals? What obstacles block the way? What can we do to overcome these obstacles?
* Why do we (I) deserve to be a national, conference, game contender? What do we (I) need to do to act like a contender?
* What is it like to compete against us (me)? How does our (my) opponent need to prepare for us (me)?

Evolved individuals put themselves last, yet they are first.
Selflessness ultimately ushers in personal fulfillment.
✳ Deng Ming-Dao, *Tao Wisdom*

I N CHAPTER 10, you learned that Sun-Tzu believed the key to victory in battle was unity of purpose and heart. At the root of this unity is the virtue of selflessness, an unconditional willingness to put the team or group before any individual or self needs.

In athletics or business, championlike teams have a high degree of unity, which is dependent on the selflessness of each of their members. Individualism detracts from team excellence; selflessness brings personal and collective fulfillment, creates peace, and conserves energy, all of which contribute to higher levels of play. As you will begin to see, the most important question to ask as a champion is not "What can I get? Points, goals, attention, recognition?" The deeper, more relevant question is "How can I give? To my team, coach, sport, opponent?"

In a society of achievers, most tend to be self-absorbed, with a more selfish "What can I get?" attitude. Such an approach to life is contrary to nature, to the Tao, which teaches that when you give you will receive. Rather than get, try to give. Be kind, caring, and generous. This is a champion. Such athletes make those around them greater. Jordan, Gretsky, Montana, Pelé are perfect examples of the selfless champion.

Selflessness is an essential ingredient in team harmony, and that's why I devoted an entire chapter to this virtue. Here's what two well-known writers have said about selflessness.

Walt Whitman wrote, "When I give, I give to myself." Giving to others takes us away from ourselves and either puts our own difficulties entirely aside or at least helps us gain a better perspective.

In his book *Man's Search for Meaning*, Viktor Frankl gives us a vivid, dramatic example of the spiritual sustenance provided by being selfless. While incarcerated in a Hitler death camp, Frankl noted that the people who kept their strength and sanity the longest were not the ones who managed by force or cleverness to obtain more than their share of scarce food. Instead it was those who aided other prisoners and shared selflessly with them the little food they had. Their physical and mental condition seemed to be strengthened by their selflessness and kindness, by the focus they placed on their fellow prisoners rather than themselves. The outcome is no different when champions adopt this virtue as a way of being with a team.

SURRENDERING SELF-INTEREST

The strength of the pack is the wolf and the strength of the wolf is the pack.

✳ Rudyard Kipling

ACCORDING TO THE TAO, those who place themselves last will be brought forward. The soul of a team or group is established in an environment of unselfishness. The strength of any team is the byproduct of its group members' willingness to modulate their enthusiasm for personal gain. Lao-Tzu encourages action without self-interest. In a society where there's a premium on individual achievement, it's not easy to get beyond self-indulgence.

You may recall the exciting play of the USA women's soccer team in World Cup competition. They were able to set self-interest aside. Following their victory over China for the world championship, we learned how they each accepted diminished roles, refused to gripe, and were willing to do anything they were asked. Placing self-interest aside for the greater good of the team was a big factor in their sweet success. They had what the Tao calls *tz'u*, which means caring for others' performance.

As I said in the opening of this chapter, and I believe it's worth repeating here, the problem for many athletes is that they are, by nature, achievers, and achievers ask the question: "What can I get?" not "How can I give?" The paradox is that true achievement is attained by giving. Notice what happens in your life when you continue to give to others. You can't stop them from giving back. Rather than ask: "How can I get more points, goals, rebounds, assists?" ask "How can I give more support to my teammates, more time and effort in practice?"

Phil Jackson understands the Tao paradox that when you let go of the need to get, you will receive in great abundance. As head coach of the NBA Chicago Bulls and Los Angeles Lakers, he had to develop two superstars who were racking up the points each night but never won a world championship. On two separate occasions, he asked Michael Jordan and Shaquille O'Neal to consider giving to their teams, to contribute by helping others to raise the level of their game, to help bring out the best in their teammates. Both athletes "bought into" this request from their warrior leader, and the very next season they led their team to the world championship and were unanimously voted MVP for the entire season.

Bill Bradley, basketball star with Princeton University and the New York Knicks, knows about the impact of selflessness on winning two world championships. In his beautiful book, *Values of the Game*, Bradley claims that "championships are not won unless a team has forged a high degree of unity, attainable only through the selflessness of each of its players. Untrammeled individualism destroys the chance for achieving victory."

Strange but true, when the name on the front of the jersey is more important than the name on the back, magic happens. When you shift from a "me" focus to a "we" consciousness, you achieve much more. I'm not sure where I heard this, but I use it often: T.E.A.M. is an acronym for "together everyone achieves more."

Surrendering self-interest is similar to a good investment. Invest in your team, in each other. As the "heart" account grows, and you refuse to withdraw from it for selfish purposes, you accumulate dividends payable down the road. The rewards are certain; you just need to trust.

And trusting this is not easy for any of us. It's natural to fear that you won't get what you deserve. You might even feel insecure, jealous, or even angry at others. But in time, you will begin to see that this higher road of selflessness and giving is the one you will always want to take. Yet in sports, business, and life, you will be tested frequently on this topic. Know that you will never master the art of service and giving. Just try to be more conscious of it and serve more often.

When you find yourself hesitating to give, for whatever reason, think about this story: The most selfless act one can perform is to risk one's own life trying to save the life of another. When San Antonio Spurs star Sean Elliot was in dire need of a kidney transplant, his brother Noel selflessly stepped up and saved Sean's life.

UNCONDITIONAL SERVICE

GOOD TEAMS have good servants. According to an old Chinese saying, "To rule is to serve, and to serve is to rule." By taking on a role of service, you nurture the environment and help create an effective group or team. You serve by doing and giving... doing what is expected and giving it your all.

The word *samurai* in Japanese means servant. The samurai warrior knew that by serving others, all was possible. As champions, you can take this to heart by serving your teammates your best shot, best move, best defensive posture, best all-out effort. In this way, you give to them the opportunity to become better, to raise their levels. Give them your passion, your integrity, your courage, your tenacity. Challenge each other in ways that make it so difficult that everyone improves. Refuse to let up.

Like the samurai warrior, give your loyalty, respect, patience, and acceptance of differences. Give to others, who you are and what you represent. In these ways, all benefit, including yourself.

Prior to each practice, game, or meeting, answer the question "How can I best serve my team, coach, group, or opponent today?"

In order to best serve, you must know your role. When your role is clear, giving is an offshoot of that role. Good leaders and coaches make sure that all players and group members have well-defined roles that can be demonstrated. Your role may be to come off the bench with high energy in order to give your team a boost. Maybe your role is to play tenacious defense in a game, or to be a tough practice player every day. If your role is unclear, ask those in charge. Your contribution is important, and if you do it well, you are a champion.

Think of a beautiful, powerful Porsche. It has a terrific, strong, high-functioning engine that runs the car. Then there are the wheels, whose role is to enable the car to move smoothly on the road. Without them, the car doesn't go. If you lose a lug nut, the car is essentially immobilized. The windshield helps you to see clearly by keeping the rain and snow from hitting your face. Without the wipers, you come to a halt. Everything has a role, equally as important. The driver, in this case, is the coach. The best, strongest, most powerful engine goes nowhere without the key, the wheel, the oil, or gas. A good team functions like a good car. Your role, whatever it is, is crucial to the overall mission of the team. You are vital—and never forget that.

> *All have a role whether it's the head, tail, or guts; all respond to help based on what's needed . . . for the good of the team, be willing to do anything.*
>
> ✱ Sun-Tzu

Perhaps you want to serve in a different way from your specified role. Maybe you want more playing time. While you fulfill your present role, go to the coach or powers that be and ask the question: "How can I change my role to playing more minutes, playing a different position, having more responsibility in the organization?" Find out what it takes, and give it your all.

PLAYING SECOND FIDDLE

BEING A TEAM PLAYER on the bench is not easy. I mentioned earlier that sometimes, if you're not playing in a game, you'll feel insecure, envious, jealous, and angry. These are natural feelings. You may even hope that those you love will fail or get injured. We all have these thoughts. You must accept them and put them aside and cheer anyway. Focus on your vital contribution, the important role you do play, and make sure you are ready to go in and step up if someone gets hurt or is not doing the job. Then, continue to give teammates the best opponent in practice, without which, the team wouldn't get better.

How many minutes you play, or how many jobs you're assigned at work, or how much you are paid should be no indication of how much you are valued. A good coach and team's commitment to you should be the same as it is to all others, regardless of minutes played—and that commitment is to facilitate your total development as an athlete, and as a person as well. You must realize that not all players are equal in terms of their commitment to the sport.

If all were treated equally with regard to playing time, that would undermine those who make a deeper commitment. So, if you are in this position of wanting more playing time, you need to:

1. Give yourself adequate time to develop; have patience.

2. Talk with your coach: "What might I do differently?"

3. Are you willing to pay your dues (be involved, encourage others, serve the team, work more)?

4. Make the most of your situation and see what the future holds for you. Decide what's worth it and go from there.

5. Understand that there's more to being part of a team than minutes. Discover what that is and decide if it is enough.

6. Do the best you can do and see where that takes you.

I will tell you that I played second fiddle early on in my career before getting my chance at center stage. I initially fought it . . . thought I deserved better. In retrospect, I now understand that I needed to mature, improve, and evolve into a first stringer in my professional game. I achieved it the old fashioned way—I earned it, through lots of practice and hard work. I became, over time, willing to do anything I was asked to do, regardless of what it would take to be good and to get the recognition I deserved. My heart and soul were employed for this purpose.

ONENESS OF VISION

TEAM SPIRIT is enhanced and strengthened through the efforts of everyone working together for a unified purpose. Selflessness promotes this "oneness of vision," a healthy collaborative association that strives for a spiritual togetherness of uniting hearts and minds. The *Tao Te Ching* reminds us of how the Earth and Heaven merge and cooperate to create soft rains and gentle flowers. So it is in athletics and life, as team or group members come together, one heart, one mind, to create higher, more proficient levels of play. Corporations, families, and other connected groups join together to reap the benefits of selfless, cooperative action while "raising the barn" together.

Selfless teams cooperate with coaching strategies and fellow teammates. The Chinese calligraphic symbol for cooperation represents a oneness of vision sharing one heart and one reason. This idea is blemished in environments where individuals are self-centered and absorbed in "me" rather than "we."

Another characteristic of selfless teams is their sense of interdependence, the notion of one for all and all for one. In Chinese, it is called *hsiang sheng,* or "mutual arising." This is a way of creating stronger mutual support when the going gets tough; and, because of this connectedness, the tough, indeed, get going together. Teams and groups aligned with this principle of mutual fulfillment become like family, intimately related to one another, connected within the greater whole to something much bigger than any one member.

Selfless, unified, and connected athletes or business partners perform at higher levels. I think about my work over the last ten years with the University of Maryland's women's lacrosse and field hockey teams, winners of numerous national championships. It's no accident that those who have had oneness of vision, selflessness, and cooperative, connected efforts are those who became crowned champions, able to demonstrate high levels of performance day after day. Creating successful teams is, indeed, a spiritual act of forgoing self-indulgence for the higher purpose of team, clan, family.

Sun-Tzu believed that victory is ultimately the byproduct of unity of purpose and heart. It goes beyond simple winning on the scoreboard. Such connectedness creates emotional and spiritual victory in the development of strong bonds and the discovery of our unlimited potential. It's comforting when you begin to create the awareness that everything in life is connected. The tree provides the paper for the author to use for writing; books teach others to care for the trees; the Earth and the Heavens exist for each other, and, therefore, they are eternal.

LESSONS AS AFFIRMATIONS

* The question to ask each day is: "How can I give today?"
* When I let go of my need to get, I receive in great abundance.
* Together, we all achieve more.
* I accept my role; my heart and soul are in it.
* My value to my team is related to so much more than how much I play.
* With patience, I give myself time to develop; I make the most of the situation.
* Cooperation and connectedness are crucial to strong teams and organizations.
* I look for all the ways in which we are interconnected, and as a result, we experience mutual fulfillment.

QUESTIONS ON THE QUEST:

* What four specific actions or behaviors will help me demonstrate how to give to my team, group, or family?
* What is my role on this team, in this organization, and what do I need to do to fulfill it?
* How am I being selfish each day? What do I need to do today to demonstrate selflessness in my relationships?

12. Lessons on Conscious Leadership

One whose humanitarian care extends to all under his command, whose trustworthiness and justice win the allegiance of neighboring nations . . . who regards all as his family, is a great leader who cannot be opposed.
        ✳ Zhuge Liang, Chinese strategist

CONSCIOUS LEADERSHIP is the delicate art of listening to others' needs so that you may serve with respect, trust, and modesty. Average leaders feel the need to promote their own agenda, talk incessantly about directives, and expect others to follow blindly. They are intent upon micromanagement, an antiquated leadership technique based on obedience and fear. The Tao teaches us that champion leaders are those whose existence is merely known, those who are standing in the background, refusing to take credit for victory yet accepting the responsibility for defeat.

Sun-Tzu's vision of a champion leader is one of a leader who refrains from reckless, forceful behavior, from being too cautious, from being short-tempered; good leaders, according to *The Art of War*, exert control by keeping emotions in check and refusing to constantly interfere with others' performance. Effective, conscious leaders remain calm, collected, and controlled amid chaos. Yet, in sport, I see coaches and team captains defeat their purpose by using control and force as methods of leading, which creates tension, self-doubt, and loss of confidence and focus in the players. Such a forceful style creates a sense of alienation, resistance, and

ultimately resentment throughout the team. Even Napoleon believed, as he aged, in the inability of force to create anything. In the long run, the sword is always beaten by the spirit, to use his words.

> *There is a need to have good leaders. Incompetent leaders compromise the strength of the group allowing lesser groups to take charge and win. Take time to establish great leadership.*
>
> ✳ Sun-Tzu

I am witnessing much change occurring in sports, business, and life. People are demanding champion leadership, as described by Zhuge Liang in the opening words of this chapter. Champion leaders understand that if you treat others humanely, with respect, encouragement, compassion, and firmness, you enhance the chances of victory. When others are consciously led, they approach their leader for advice, demonstrate unwavering loyalty, and offer dedicated obedience. When you lead in this way, you win the hearts of others as they take upon themselves the hardship, sacrifice, and suffering so crucial to the attainment of goals. Athletes, business associates, and family members in these environments simply choose to give a little more than they thought was possible.

Champion leadership, I have learned, also demands a tender touch, treating others with love and kindness, while at the same time being firm when pointing out where changes need to be made. Coach John Wooden would tell people that part of his huge success was due to the fact that there was a lot of love in his coaching.

When there is doubt about this path, remind yourself about one unquestionable fact: In most circumstances, those you lead are volunteers. Without them, you have no one to lead. Treat them well.

ART OF CHOOSING LEADERS

OVER THE YEARS, I have learned that the selection of team or group leaders is no easy task. It is a process complicated by many variables. I have used the following exercise as an educational tool to help athletes to tune in to the essence of solid leadership, and successfully select candidates who exemplify such fine qualities.

First of all, divide your team or group into smaller groups of four to ten people, depending on how large the team is. Ask the groups to appoint one person to record information as it's received. Now, ask the groups to list what they believe to be the specific qualities essential to conscious, effective leadership. Words like loyal, dependable, insightful, caring, strong, vocal, confident, fearless, and calm might appear. When the list is complete, ask the recorder of each group to announce the qualities, while someone from the staff records them on a board, visible to all. Repeated or overlapping qualities are discarded. When the "mas-

ter" list is created, ask for comments. Once the list is finalized, ask each member to act alone and list anonymously, on a sheet of paper, the names of three people on the team who best exemplify these traits, number one being the best. Collect the sheets, tally the results at another time, and use the information to help select team leaders and captains. The names more often than not will align with a coach's intuitive selection and confirm what he or she already knew would be the best choice. If that is not the case, this information should help you to see something you are missing. This method accomplishes two things: First, the team feels that they had a say in the process, and second, it eliminates the selection of captains based on unreliable, unrelated reasons such as looks, talent, age, class, or popularity. The experience, as I have said, is an educational tool, instructing everyone about what champion leadership is all about. For example, champion leaders lead most effectively, not by ordering or telling others what to do, but by getting involved, encouraging others, setting a good example, and showing respect, courtesy, and loyalty to others. They lead by serving teammates during practice by playing in a way that makes it difficult and challenging for them. They offer the best they have, with the result that they all become better athletes because of their all-out efforts. That's true leadership. These leaders display integrity, loyalty, dignity, courage, compassion, patience, and the willingness to suffer for the higher good . . . the team, family, tribe.

From my experience working with teams that display strong leadership, the common ground is that they buy into the notion that leadership is everyone's role. To help others see themselves as leaders, ask all members to choose three or four of the traits up on the board that they think they could exhibit. Once they choose these traits, ask that they list three or four behaviors or actions that, if performed, would demonstrate those traits of being an effective leader. You will be pleasantly surprised to experience leadership spreading throughout the ranks. If you're not acting as leaders in this way, you are hurting your team. You can begin to earn respect as a leader now by leading in these ways.

THE GUIDING WAY

> *Tao guides with the Watercourse Way. It uses little intervention, no manipulation, no coercion. Shed light to show the path. Suggest choices and they will say, "We did it ourselves!"*
>
> ✳ *Tao Te Ching*

THE WATERCOURSE WAY is the Way of the Champion. The champion leads by guidance rather than by control. Being a "control freak" is indicative of various levels of insecurity. As the Buddha knows, if you want to truly control the cows, move the fences back; open things up, give more space for others to grow, explore, and find a way to discover their own greatness.

As I have learned, the champion leader wants to guide—not direct—others to become more self-reliant. Control blocks self-reliance, vision, and creativity. For example, if you are an expert fisherman, rather than catch fish for the village and teach them to become dependent on your presence, try to guide and free them by teaching them how to fish, so they will always have food in your absence. With athletes, you want them to be creative and do it themselves while alone on the field or court. Guidance without excessive control is the way to help others realize their potential.

The Chinese symbol for control honors the way of letting be, allowing nature to prevail through loving guidance. Only when you are willing to let go of excessive control (which happens when you are secure within yourself) will you, your team, and others enjoy true learning and victory.

Confucius says that the great leader "guides others and does not pull them along; urges them to go forward by opening the way, yet refuses to take them to the place."

I have learned the following from champion leaders, and this will help you be a more conscious guide for those you lead to places of improvement and growth:

✸ Be open to listening to criticism from others, particularly if it is the opinion of the majority. As a coach, corporate executive, or head of a household, show them your openness to feedback by asking them periodically (especially during times of tension and disharmony) to respond in writing to the question: "If you were in charge and had complete freedom to handle things your way, what would you do and how would you do it?" They should respond to this question anonymously, in order to ensure honest and truthful responses. They will respect and admire you for this, especially if you initiate positive change based on their suggestions and criticisms.

✸ Create an open, positive environment where all feel accepted, respected, and able to grow as individuals. Be fair; show no favoritism to the "stars." For example, all athletes or members of the team should work equally hard. With regard to the guidelines for team or group conduct, be consistent. Team members appreciate behavior boundaries, which foster a sense of security. But within that structure, be sure to give them the freedom to develop and be themselves.

✸ Before you criticize those you lead, first look for ways to give them credit. For example, you can say, "Sonia, I love the way you always hustle. Now, if you want to kick it up a notch, use your hands like this, and shuffle your feet at the same time." By the time you criticize her arms and footwork, she is ready to listen, knowing you acknowledge her work ethic. Be sure to provide concrete, specific data for your critique. Avoid gross generalizations such as "you always" or "you never." Search for ways that you, together with the athlete, coworker, or family member, can address the problem. Suggestions coming from them will hold more weight, and compliance will come more easily. When feasible, don't criticize during a performance. Your comments will be more effective if you wait and introduce them at the next practice session or on the next day.

✸ As a coach or team leader, you need to understand that your position is only as strong and secure as you make your athletes feel. The players or workers can make you or break you.

✳ If you demonstrate a sincere willingness to help and serve others, they will approach you for advice and guidance. If you are willing to listen to others, they will be attracted to you and partake in a wonderful exchange of ideas.

✳ Avoid manipulation at all costs. As a leadership style, it creates anger, resentment, and loss of respect on the part of those it's used against. Power plays, trying to exert your position over others, and being "the boss" are a form of manipulation that creates environments of distrust and suspicion. Motivation and team spirit diminish with the use of such tactics.

✳ Remember the Golden Rule: "Treat others as you would like to be treated." If you follow this rule, your problems will be minimized. Harshness gets you nowhere?why use it? When you are kind to others, you win their hearts and cooperation, which is what you really want and deserve. (See the next lesson, "Firm Yet Fair.")

✳ Create environments where setbacks, mistakes, errors, and failures are permissible. In this way, people will take risks to explore their unlimited potential, without fear of judgment or criticism upon any failure.

In these ways you nourish your followers. The *I Ching* clearly tells us that when the rulers nourish the ruled, they will watch them bring out their talents.

FIRM YET FAIR

HIS NAME WAS HUGH LYNCH, one of the most fearless and highly respected chiefs in the New York City Fire Department. People under his command said how brave he was, leading dozens of men, half his age, into the belly of a raging fire. He led by example and guided others to places they needed to be, as is characteristic of a champion leader. They listened to him because, as one fireman stated, he was firm yet always fair. In this way, he was no different from my dad. I learned from this champion my first lessons on leadership.

The *I Ching* validates what my dad intuitively knew to be correct. This Tao classic states that "it is necessary that a leader have firmness and fairness with an encouraging attitude toward others." Being strict yet impartial helps a leader to be admired, honored, and obeyed.

To be firm, you need to establish certain boundaries, what will and will not be tolerated. The boundaries create a sense of security for those being led. Knowing the parameters of behavior makes for clean, predictable, and familiar circumstances. Yet within these firm boundaries, there needs to be an element of fairness—that is, treating others as they deserve to be treated.

Coach John Wooden, of the champion UCLA basketball team, knows that being fair doesn't mean treating everyone alike. That's because everyone does not earn the same treatment. In his book *Wooden*, he explains that fairness is giving to others what they earn. He also points out that being fair at all times is not possible. He encourages making a sincere effort; others will recognize that about you, whether it's your kids, employees, or athletes. Wooden was respected by his athletes, and they played their hearts out because he treated them firmly yet fairly.

To be fair in your leadership, you must refrain from making arbitrary decisions. For example, the star athlete is not given less of a punishment for wrongdoing than the athlete who hardly plays. Going outside the team boundaries—curfews, promptness, alcohol tolerance—calls for consistent consequences, regardless of one's role on the team. This is fair. And remember that with consistency of enforcement, there is order; inconsistent leadership leads to disorder. This is true whether you are a coach, team captain, CEO, or parent. Along these lines, Sun-Tzu reminds us that if you show favor or indulge others, they may become useless and unable to be directed.

LEADING WITH LOVE

THE *I Ching* makes it clear that leaders must nourish, support, and care for those led, in order to create unity within the group. Sun-Tzu alludes to the way generals would take care of the masses as one would take care of a child who was loved. By so doing, they were more likely to be victorious in their endeavors.

Once again, I lean on the leadership of coach John Wooden, winner of ten national championships in men's basketball. He equates being a coach with being a parent; your most powerful tool is love. He believes that you must love your athletes to get the most out of them, and claims that love has dominated his coaching career. As I have stated previously in this section on leadership, when asked about his consistent success, he targeted the fact that there was a lot of love in his coaching. He would criticize and "get on" his athletes, yet always remembered to couple it with a "pat on the back."

Another basketball great, coach Phil Jackson of the L.A. Lakers, leads with much love. Like a good parent, he outlines boundaries for his athletes yet is generous with his affection. In his firmness, he is sure to hold challenging players to the limits, yet they can still feel his love. This love is rooted in his strong sense of compassion, one of the champion virtues discussed in Chapter 8.

Someone once told me, and I believe it to be true, that players really don't care about what you know; they just really want to know that you care. Let those you lead in all arenas of life know how deeply you love and appreciate them. When they feel this, they will go the distance, be loyal, and do what they have been asked to do.

I carry this philosophy of leading with love to all coaches, CEOs, and other leaders whenever I present talks, workshops, or clinics on leadership. Here's what I tell others: I believe that the single most vital aspect to successful leadership is the quality of the personal relationship and love between athlete and coach, worker and manager, child and parent. When you demonstrate that you are truly invested in their success, they have a much greater chance of reaching their full potential. When you communicate your belief in them, they are more inclined to go the distance, to do all that you ask, to take appropriate risks, and to get going when the going gets tough. As a coach in athletics, you need to remember that you love your athletes and that's why you have this calling. Remember that when you lose perspective. Champion leaders and good coaches care about those they lead as individuals. They take time to know about their lives away from the athletic or work environment. They also care enough to challenge them to grow and develop as people. Good, creative leaders refuse to water things down, demanding more because they care. It demands more of you to demand more of them, and you grow as a result. You need to absolutely refuse to praise half-hearted efforts. If you do, you insult those you praise and diminish your integrity. Give them difficult tasks, while letting them know that you have confidence in their ability to do them. They need to be told that if they are not successful at first, you will be there to help them master the task. This is the real meaning of love and commitment in creative, conscious relationship. The truly great leaders and coaches that you know have this connection with their athletes, their group, their family.

THE HUMBLE HEART

> *Keep the jade and treasures subtly reserved within the bosom. A posture of humble heart will bring blessings from all directions.*
>
> ✳ *Tao Te Ching*

THE TAO strongly encourages the way of humility, to be all that you have been given, yet to act as if you have received nothing. In this way, you deflect attention toward others yet feel the blessings and compliments from everyone. For a leader, humility provides clarity when needed, while arrogance makes for cloudy vision. Humility enhances your capabilities while exposing your achievements. Basketball coach Marcus Perez, a graduate of West Point, demonstrates such humility in his leadership. He claims that in order to be a good coach, he must be willing to live without recognition. Leading, he states, is not about me as much as it is about those I lead.

Sports is an arena where many crave attention and glow with the credit for success. Many coaches and athletes feel this need to self-promote and prove their self-worth. Such attention-seeking behavior is often based on feelings of insecurity. What seems to be needed is a strong dose of humility, the ability to step aside as a leader and let others experience the accolades of success. Champion leaders understand that accomplishments are team-generated rather than the work of any one leader. The humble leader is well aware of the synergistic interdependence of all involved, where everyone shares a common goal, works together to attain it, and accepts responsibility for all outcomes.

Leaders who have an excessive need for self-promotion seem to easily overlook the needs of those they lead. When this happens, players on the team can refuse to play or to go all-out for their leader. Giving the credit to those you lead helps them to display higher levels of loyalty and respect, as they become willing to sacrifice and suffer while following the guidelines of their leader.

Another way to demonstrate humility is to encourage valuable input from those led about rules, policy, and even workouts. Many leaders fear the loss of control when soliciting such participation and resort to dictating the rules, which, paradoxically, creates disloyalty and disrespect, leading to the inevitable loss of control. Give athletes and workers a say in the organization; ask for their opinions on policy. Once this is done, they will feel very important and want to work harder to keep things in order. Remember this: most of what they suggest will usually be aligned with your objectives. If it's not, you hold the power to reject suggestions or make changes if things seem problematic.

Being humble is more potent in achieving your goals and being successful than always trying to prove yourself. Be conscious of what you do not know, and don't assume that you always have the only or the best answer; rather be open to adopting new ways of expanding your expertise. When success comes, recognize the contributions of all involved. You couldn't achieve success without the work and support of your staff, team, parents, and fans, and they couldn't do it without your guidance and expertise.

Of course, some leaders naturally attract attention and are celebrities in their own right. Yet this doesn't preclude the possibility that humility can shine through. The great ones who attract such attention—Michael Jordan, Wayne Gretsky, Tiger Woods, and others—manage to hold on to their

humble roots. But as I previously have stated, to have a sense of humility, one must have a strong concept of self and feel secure within.

WALK THE TALK

The leader embraces the One and becomes
the model for all.
  ✳ Deng Ming-Dao, *Tao Wisdom*

THE CHINESE SYMBOLS for modeling encourage you to follow in the tracks created by the wheels of a leading, guiding vehicle, much like following those who have paved the way before you on the path of the champion.

It is simple yet not so easy: As a leader, model for others exactly what you want others to model for you. For example, many coaches want their athletes to exude calmness in pressure situations. Matt Dougherty talks about the way his mentor and coach, Dean Smith, from the University of North Carolina, modeled calm in the middle of chaos: "It was during the 1982 national championship game against Georgetown. We were down one with thirty-two seconds to play, and Coach called a timeout. Here he was coaching for his first title in several attempts. Although the pressure was enormous, he spoke so calmly in that huddle that it put us in a confident mind-set as we took the court. Then some freshman named Michael Jordan smoothly hit the game-winning shot." This principle, like the Golden Rule, mirrors the Confucian ideal of the "superior leader" who models virtuous behavior.

It is important that leaders, in athletics and other arenas of performance in business and at home, be bound by the same guidelines as the team, where appropriate. For example, if you have any zero tolerance policies for the players, you might want to abide by them as well. If you expect your team to show up on time, you'd better not be tardy. If you expect them to be fit, lift weights, and run, you might consider doing the same. I love when a coach or leader joins the team in workouts. When I work with athletes, I often take them on a run up a good hill. I notice they listen more intently to my message during our locker room talks because of what I model. I like to walk my talk and lead by example. Such participation can make your credibility blossom. Remember that the strength of your influence begins with you and ripples outward.

Sportsmanship is a learned behavior. Be aware of how your actions impact others. For example, screaming at a referee or an opponent, criticizing others behind their backs or at a press conference, taunting and other demeaning actions will be imitated by those you lead. Model what you wish to teach. After all, as a leader in your competitive arena, isn't the sport or project the vehicle by which participants learn the bigger, more important lessons of life? What do you teach and how do you lead by using foul language or being intoxicated in public—falling short of the standards you demand from your athletes?

LESSONS AS AFFIRMATIONS

* I look for opportunities to treat those I lead with respect, compassion, and encouragement.
* I lead others the same way I wish to be led.
* I seek ways to guide and use less intervention.
* Micromanaging interferes with the creative process.
* I am only as strong and secure as I make others feel.
* I remain open to listening to criticism, in order to become a more effective leader.
* Be firm, be fair, and others will follow your way.
* I remain humble and give credit where credit is due.
* I always encourage input from those I lead. Because of this, I have faithful, loyal, respectful followers.
* I am aware of the power within when I model the Way of the Champion.
* If I want others to be a certain way, then I must be that way myself.

QUESTIONS ON THE QUEST:

* What four behaviors do I want others to learn, and how can I model each on a daily basis to walk my talk?
* What five traits do I consider crucial for great leadership?
* What specific actions and behaviors can I execute now in order to demonstrate those?
* What two ways can I practice a more humble approach as a champion leader?

AN EPILOGUE

Trusting the Process

Life's unfolding of events is as apparent as the coming and going of seasons; all is exactly as it is supposed to be?—trust it.
✳ Deng Ming-Dao, *Tao Wisdom*

TAO WISDOM REMINDS US to trust the river's flow. The mighty Mississippi River moves slowly at times, only to rapidly speed up in the narrows. You may even think it is reversing direction in various places, yet suddenly it turns around, heading toward its destination, the Gulf of Mexico, for a total journey of 2,348 miles. The Way of the Champion, like the river, has many reversals, setbacks, failures, and losses. You will plateau, slow down, stand still, and then speed up and experience rapid growth. There will be times when you think your progress is reversing direction, only to have it swiftly spin around and charge forward once again. All of this movement is a natural progression in your evolving process of being a champion or, as the Tao states, an unfolding of events exactly as they are supposed to be. Only the champions acknowledge, trust, and accept this natural process to be so.

When you grow flowers, you would never think about pulling them up as soon as they miraculously break through the soil, so they can grow faster and taller; you trust their growth to progress naturally. It is no different with progress on the champion's path; you must trust the process and notice the natural unfolding of events.

Refuse to give setbacks, mistakes, plateaus, or sudden reversals in sport or life permission to distract you from your mission or to make you believe you're not making progress. Know that rapid growth and advancement in any arena of performance are unusual. Change and improvement occur when the time is right, not when you think they should. When fear and self-doubt enter your nervous system, understanding this natural process will help you to have self-compassion and be kind to yourself. Remember, on your journey of being a champion, that your efforts and intuition are purposeful and filled with integrity. Try to sense the joy, beauty, and benefits of the quest, the experience itself, as a worthwhile undertaking. National champions have taught me how the journey is actually more fun and rewarding than achieving the goal.

With this new frame of heart and mind, coupled with your patient, persevering nature, like the river with all its twists, turns, and changes of direction, you will eventually find your way to the "sea" of personal greatness as you act like the champion you are in the present moment.

Olympian Wilma Rudolph had polio as a child; doctors told her that she had little chance of ever walking again without leg braces. In and out of hospitals for many of her early years, while enduring major setbacks, fears, and doubts, she refused to follow the opinions of experts, choosing instead to trust her own instincts. She defeated this disease and went on to win three Olympic gold medals. Like Wilma, you are capable of extraordinary things when you trust and believe in this process of being a champion.

And, please trust the value of joyful laughter on your journey. Many good athletes and accomplished businesspeople take themselves too seriously; they seem to lack fun because they are so anxious or stressed about the possibility of failing or making mistakes. Good humor helps to promote well-being and optimal performance. Trust me, not to laugh at one's failures is costly, a setup for more failure. It makes for a tight, tense, and tentative performance. Don't confuse laughter and humor with a lack of seriousness. Be serious in your pursuit and preparation, but laugh at the absurdity when setback, loss, or failure take you off guard. Laughter will adjust your lens of perception with regard to all outcomes and results.

I want to remind you that progress on this journey may slow down like the river. No need to panic or be fearful. Remain trustful of the Way of the Champion. As I said earlier, events and circumstances in life often cause much tension and stress when they unfold contrary to how we think they should. A champion knows that things happen as they are supposed to, according to the way of nature, the Way of the Champion, the Watercourse Way.

The following bullets are going to help you to trust and become comfortable with the process, the journey itself. These morsels are taken from various sections throughout this book and offered to you at this time as reminders of how to "stay the course." Everyone gets off track; the only difference between most people and the champion is that the latter, armed with heightened awareness and consciousness, gets back on track more quickly. Use the following as affirmations, "champion finger food," when you become distracted along the way:

❋ Nothing gargantuan is ever needed . . . just be who you are.

❋ Don't try to dominate a situation; simply demonstrate your greatness.

❋ It's really about "us"—can we raise our bar by using the opponent?

❋ Exhibit a presence; stay connected to the right stuff, and fill up the arena with your spirit.

❋ In the joy of going all-out, I forget my pain.

* Opponents will look in my eyes; what they see may determine the outcome of the game or meeting.

* Talent counts, yet the champion knows that it's usually about who has the most heart.

* Don't try to fight your opponent; fight to uphold the principles and virtues of the Way of the Champion.

* Don't run away from losing; run toward winning, doing all the little things that create big things.

* Know the difference between what you can and can't control; take charge of what you can, and let go of the rest.

* Don't need to be the best; just be the best you can be right now.

* Forget outcomes and focus on this positive opportunity given to you.

* An archer shooting for the love of shooting has all the skill; when shooting for gold, the archer goes blind.

* What message do you want to send to your opponent? What do you need to specifically do to make sure it's received?

In sports, as in life, one thing is certain: SHIFT HAPPENS! Change is inevitable, like it or not. While some shifts or changes are tangible, such as skill development or body mass, other shifts tend to be intangible, impacting the mental, emotional, and spiritual aspects of performance. Such inner shifts of the heart-mind (*hsing* in Chinese) remind me of the Zen Buddhist monk who approaches a street hot-dog vendor and gently asks, "Sir, please make me one with everything." The vendor looks at him strangely and proceeds to load the hot dog with several condiments. Receiving his purchase, the monk hands over a twenty-dollar bill for the two-dollar item. The vendor says "Thank you" and waits on another person. After waiting patiently for a few minutes, the monk finally says to the vendor, "Sir, what about change?" The man replies, "Oh, yes, my friend . . . change. As you probably know, change comes from within."

And so it is with the Way of the Champion. The change you experience on this journey will come from within and ripple outward to all things in your life. This quest, which no one can undertake for you, is an inner one filled with wisdom, very private, and deeply personal. Marcel Proust, a brilliant and important French novelist of the last century, says that there are two methods of obtaining such wisdom: painlessly from a teacher or painfully from life; the latter is far superior. That said, I do not pretend to teach you wisdom. You must learn it for yourself on this champion's journey. I simply offer you this handy, practical guide to help you stay the course as you embark on these unchartered waters. Practice these sacred lessons of champions, lessons on mental strength, conscious leadership, and true winning in your sport, business, or home. Let this book comfort you along "the Way."

Fasten your seat belt and get ready for some fun-filled shifts.

ABOUT THE AUTHORS

Jerry Lynch, Ph. D, is an internationally recognized sports psychologist, speaker, coach and national-class athlete who has taught at Penn State, Colorado, Stanford, and Santa Clara universities. Over the past twenty-five years, Jerry has worked with hundreds of championship teams and athletes in the U.S. and abroad. He is also the author of eight books including the perennial bestseller, *Thinking Body, Dancing Mind* (with Chungliang Al Huang). Dr. Lynch can be contacted by visiting his website: www.wayofthechampions.com.

Chungliang Al Huang is founder and president of the Living Tao Foundation and the Lan Ling Institute in China. He is an internationally recognized authority on the Tao, a Tai Ji master, a calligrapher and the author of many books, including the bestselling *Embrace Tiger, Return To Mountain.*